Random House
summer nights
crosswords

edited by Stanley Newman

Random House
Puzzles & Games

NEW YORK   TORONTO   LONDON   SYDNEY   AUCKLAND

Visit the Random House Puzzles & Games Web site:
www.puzzlesatrandom.com

First Edition

Printed in the United States of America

10 9 8 7 6 5 4

ISBN: 978-0-8129-3627-8

Introduction

Welcome to *Random House Summer Nights Crosswords,* with 100 sweet and sassy puzzles from some of America's most talented puzzlemakers. Each crossword has a theme, or central idea, running through its longest answers. The title provided at the top of each page will give you a hint as to what the theme is. And the answers are all in the back, just in case.

Thanks to Oriana Leckert and Lance Nathan for their help in the preparation of the manuscript.

Your comments on any aspect of this book are most welcome. You can reach me via regular mail or e-mail at the addresses below.

If you're Internet-active, you're invited to my Web site, www.StanXwords.com. It features puzzlemaker profiles, solving hints and other useful info for crossword fans. There's also a free daily crossword and weekly prize contest. Please stop by for a visit.

Best wishes for happy solving!

Stan Newman

Regular mail: P.O. Box 69, Massapequa Park, NY 11762
(Please enclose a self-addressed stamped envelope if you'd like a reply.)

E-mail: StanXwords@aol.com

Join Stan Newman on His Annual Crossword-Theme Cruise!

You'll enjoy a relaxing vacation on a luxurious ship, plus a full program of puzzles, games, and instructional sessions. For complete info on Stan's next cruise, please phone Special Event Cruises at 1-800-326-0373, or visit its Web site, www.specialeventcruises.com/crossword.html.

1 HOW OFTEN?

by Bob Lubbers

ACROSS

1 Slander
7 Printer's widths
10 Will-o'-the-__
14 Mrs. Rocky Balboa
15 Barnyard sound
16 Singer __ James
17 9-to-5, for many
19 Merit
20 Trumpeted
21 Swiss painter
22 __ War (1850s conflict)
26 Shows age, as newspaper
28 Gram starter
29 High degree
31 Dissenting vote
32 Ugandan exile
33 *The Naked and the __*
35 Ski run
39 Ushers
41 Deli bread
42 Skin cleanser
43 Chocolate-flavored coffee
44 Min. parts
46 Stadium row
47 Vietnam Memorial architect
49 *Krazy __*
50 Carry
51 Nebuchad-nezzar's realm
55 Like a hawk
57 Ended
58 Teacher's protection
60 Remove, to an editor
61 Club cost
66 Ireland's nickname
67 W. Va. summer setting
68 Forever, old-style
69 Opposite of 60 Across
70 Mao __-tung
71 Muscle-bone connector

DOWN

1 June honoree
2 Author LeShan
3 Part of TGIF
4 Feel off
5 Perhaps
6 Merrie Olde __
7 Persian Gulf ruler
8 Long green
9 Soaked
10 State-run game
11 Aviator Balbo
12 Disseminate
13 Stamp sheets
18 They carry on
22 Abyss
23 Loverboy
24 Leg artery
25 Tenant's responsiblity
27 Endure
30 *Wild Wild West* actress
34 Illinois city
36 Pungent plant
37 Pro golfer Calvin
38 Strayed
40 Spinnaker, e.g.
45 Movie hopeful
48 Later, maybe
51 Portends
52 Stave off
53 Contradict
54 Requirements
56 Island of MacArthur's return
59 Hoopster Archibald
62 Cub Scout group
63 Norse fate goddess
64 Rock producer Brian
65 Yen fraction

2 THEY DONE IT

....

by Rich Norris

ACROSS

1 Breathe heavily
5 Payment option
9 Type of beam
14 Inventor's starting point
15 Cream-filled cookie
16 Bizarre
17 Charlie Chan's creator
20 Car on a train
21 Anjou relative
22 Denver hrs.
23 Koblenz complaint
25 Deli side dish
27 Wise one
31 "__ Woman" (Reddy song)
33 Puts up with
37 Model-train layout
38 Heavy load
40 Not up to the task
41 Philip Marlowe's creator
44 Floor worker
45 Stay away from
46 Bread spread
47 Cautionary signals
49 Six-time NL home run champ
50 Stinging insect
51 Pillow cover
53 "__ who?"
55 Rainbow shape
58 Tram loads
60 Save
65 Dr. Gideon Fell's creator
68 Dispatch boat
69 "See you later!"
70 Like some testimony
71 Impose a second levy on
72 Tiny particle
73 Long story

DOWN

1 Slapstick missiles
2 Seth's dad
3 Pianist Peter
4 Lecture
5 Force
6 LAX posting
7 Balkan War participant
8 Rail riders
9 Lincoln's birthplace
10 Summer mo.
11 Wineglass feature
12 Messes up
13 What's left
18 Narc's employer: Abbr.
19 Majorca, for *una*
24 Card-game holdings
26 Look-out device?
27 In a way
28 Be of use
29 Singer Crystal
30 Glue name
32 Many, in Madrid
34 Street of fiction
35 Foil relatives
36 Barber-chair attachment
39 Closes
42 Generally approved
43 Waiting area
48 Draped garment
52 Tourist attraction
54 Eastern discipline
55 Not quite closed
56 Wander about
57 Receipt, informally
59 Revue offering
61 Glasgow resident
62 Irene of *Fame*
63 Russia's __ Mountains
64 Agatha contemporary
66 Govt. hush-hush group
67 __ Paulo

3 THEATER IN THE ROUND?

by Richard Silvestri

ACROSS

1 Loot
5 Things to do
10 Arnold and Watson
14 Succotash bean
15 Key
16 Corn product
17 Start of a question from George Carlin
20 Comprehensive
21 Salad type
22 Scholarly time?
23 Satirical piece
24 Has to offer
28 Mexican export
29 Madrid Mrs.
32 Smithy sight
33 Tater
34 Prepared for a drive
35 Part 2 of the question
38 Heedless
39 Pull down
40 Present at birth
41 A little flat?
42 Infection suppressants
43 Flasher of a sort
44 Candle holder
45 Sault __ Marie, MI
46 Put off
49 Arabian cloak
54 End of the question
56 Slight in structure
57 "Blowin' in the Wind" composer
58 Draft status
59 Can't stand
60 Loose talk?
61 __ out (scraped by)

DOWN

1 Performed a glissade
2 Not a single woman
3 Last of a loving threesome
4 Dressy event
5 Bibliography info
6 Far from florid
7 Downhill racer
8 Garden spot of London
9 Place for prisoners
10 Ready for renters
11 Ransom of note
12 Big butte
13 Rise high
18 Like a singing Richard
19 Commuter line
23 Treat with contempt
24 Iraqi port
25 Saloon sign
26 "Cease!" at sea
27 Sorrowful sound
28 Wagnerian work
29 Fray
30 Therapy, for a GI
31 Ginger's predecessor
33 Wall Street unit
34 Pre-Soviet monarch
36 Getaway times
37 Aim
42 Bullpen success
43 Sequence
44 Poetic region
45 Brooke's sitcom role
46 Miss America accessory
47 Islands entertainment
48 Clean up copy
49 Hungarian name
50 Oklahoma tribesman
51 Cry from the sty
52 Old dagger
53 "Zounds!"
55 One-eighth of a V-8: Abbr.

4 TO COIN A PHRASE

by Lee Weaver

ACROSS

1 Central point
6 Goes ashore
13 Light-sensitive device
14 Piano keys, slangily
15 Arm art
16 __ point (viewing place)
17 Considerable sum
20 Sly looks
21 Makes mistakes
22 Three-strikes result
25 Eve's garden
26 "How sweet __!"
27 Notched, as a leaf
29 Commonplace
31 Merriment
35 Most pleasant
36 Metal coating
40 Wise saying
41 Emerald Isle
42 Masticate
46 Sunbather's goal
47 Ancient Briton
48 Harvest wool
49 Livestock herder's mount
52 Rise again
55 Military pilots
56 Map collections
57 Slow-moving mollusks
58 Periods of great success
59 Attacks with snowballs

DOWN

1 Piled up
2 Main dish
3 To the rear, at sea
4 Kunta Kinte's story
5 Quick gait
6 Of various kinds
7 Actress Dame Edith
8 German city
9 Pretentious
10 River inlet
11 Beer barrel
12 U-turn from NNW
13 Less than fresh
18 Abominable Snowman
19 Stiffly precise
22 Seep
23 Applications
24 Camper's shelter
26 Pastoral poem
27 Singer Adams
28 Sinbad's transport
29 Suit to __
30 Poker ritual
31 Pesky insect
32 Verdi heroine
33 "__ See Clearly Now"
34 Cardiology test: Abbr.
37 Noblewoman
38 Cheerful song
39 Johnson of *Laugh-In*
42 For a group of singers
43 Loner
44 Art-studio stands
45 Small songbirds
47 Shrewd
48 "Rise and __!"
49 Campus area, for short
50 Bear: Lat.
51 Wood file
52 Pep-rally yell
53 Summer, in Bordeaux
54 Like a fox

5 SEW WHAT?

by Bob Lubbers

ACROSS

1 Adherent's suffix
4 Lyric poets
10 Ottoman official
14 Russian space station
15 Hindu incantation
16 Percussion instrument
17 "What Kind of Fool __?"
18 Saul's kingdom
19 Architect Saarinen
20 Zing
23 Seven-year-old's sch.
24 Brown pigment
27 Inhibit
29 Swiss river
32 __ *Is Born*
33 Never-ending
36 "... __ I saw Elba"
37 Go around obstacles
41 __-Magnon
42 Actress Arquette
43 Lubricated
46 On a pension: Abbr.
47 Egg-shaped
51 Steeples
53 Art Deco artist
54 1939 Van Heusen tune
60 Memorable time periods
62 Speechmaker
63 Pie __ mode
64 Funny Martha
65 Titanium ore
66 Uproar
67 Legendary loch
68 Tried
69 Joyless

DOWN

1 Formed a concept
2 Metaphor kin
3 Hot-dish mount
4 Leave out
5 Short race
6 Concerning
7 Ollie's pal
8 Forest element
9 Bargain events
10 Astaire and Simpson
11 Hot drink
12 *Ben-__*
13 Latin 101 word
21 Kuwaiti ruler
22 Spanish day
25 Not any
26 "You __ My Sunshine"
28 Highway: Abbr.
29 Passion
30 Win by __
31 Attacked
34 Corn serving
35 Author Deighton
37 Stumble
38 Christmas and Easter
39 __-cone (icy treat)
40 Semaphore sender
41 Army execs.
44 Removes
45 __ *Spiegel*
48 Mountain nymphs
49 Where *Firenze* is
50 Insist upon
52 Bull sound
55 Undeniable
56 They're often checked at dinner
57 Have a go __
58 Enameled lacquerware
59 The __ Scott Decision
60 Sea eagle
61 Actress Charlotte

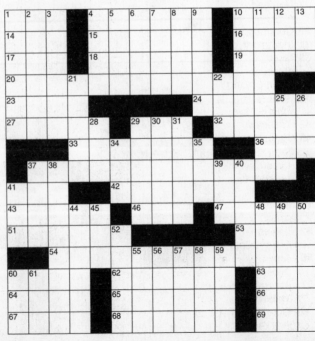

6 TAKE YOUR MEDICINE

by Patrick Jordan

ACROSS

1 Bit of bunco
5 Overhead sight at a ballgame
10 __ California
14 Folk singer Guthrie
15 Sound portion
16 Actor Stoltz
17 It's often certified
18 Whitecap
19 Where Wile E. gets his gadgets
20 Leaving speedily
23 Oktoberfest vessels
24 Wholly absorbed
28 Woodland deity
30 Newspaper story
31 Culp/Cosby series
34 Brimless topper
36 Compete against Tommy Moe
37 Bunkhouse bunk
38 Prefix for laryngology
39 Sold off quickly
44 Cow's hurdle, in rhyme
45 Burst forth
46 Singer McEntire
48 Increase
49 Lead actor in *The Wizard of Oz*
53 Apollo vehicle
57 Lugosi of fright film fame
60 Dangerous gas
61 Privileged person
62 Malevolence
63 Gave it a go
64 Enthusiastic

65 Mediterranean seaport
66 Gravity-powered toys
67 Lacking, in Lyons

DOWN

1 One of the Greek 31 Down
2 Ceramics or macramé
3 "Get __!" ("Move on!")
4 Placate
5 Corroborates
6 Tackle-box item
7 Vague impression
8 Fail to attend
9 Mint or thyme
10 Kiddie-lit author Potter
11 Rainbow shape
12 Comical Carrey
13 Star pitcher
21 "__ pig's eye!"
22 Aware of
25 "Gesundheit!" preceder
26 Student of Socrates
27 Grand __ National Park
29 Type of rechargeable battery
30 Rehem, perhaps
31 Spots of land
32 Avoid
33 Arouse one's interest
35 Sodom escapee
40 Swedish city
41 Ham __ (overact)
42 Hits the road
43 Urgent orders
44 Actress Mason et al.
47 Jazz genre
50 Jelly flavor
51 Cartoon chipmunk
52 Requirements
54 Watergate reporter Bernstein
55 Mrs. Ernie Kovacs
56 Like most universities
57 Command to canines
58 __ Marie Saint
59 Gossip columnist Smith

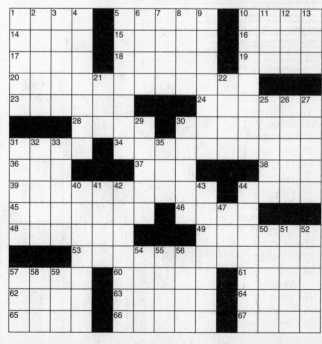

7 REMNANTS

by A.J. Santora

ACROSS

1 Meeting minimum
7 Teen dance
11 Rush or snow follower
14 Not finished
15 Gernreich of fashion
16 Marseilles water
17 Remnants
19 Brit. service decoration
20 Limestone deposit
21 Bob bait lightly
22 Something strange
24 Wide shoe
25 Fish delicacy
27 Roller-derby unit
30 Palermo pelf, in the past
31 Tresses
35 __ King's Men
38 Retired servicemen's grp.
39 "You never had __ good!"
40 Kicking out
42 Disagreeable
44 Football stadium
45 Subtraction ans.
47 Alcoves
48 Church area
49 Scurry
51 60 or so average
52 Exercise in vanity
55 Wane
58 Bleep out
61 Gstaad gear
62 Hem line, maybe
63 __ Grande
64 Gambler's concern
67 Part of a silver set
68 Blue dye
69 Oaf
70 Last letter
71 6/6/44
72 Cadres

DOWN

1 Bid proposal
2 Excessive
3 Men's organization
4 Sub __ (privately)
5 Actress Merkel
6 Patches
7 Sent an advance
8 Conduct
9 Roulette choice
10 Botch
11 Lucas returnee
12 Drying oven
13 Channel marker
18 Writer Roald
23 Burst open
26 Uninteresting
28 British stateman's family
29 Fraternity letter
32 Done with
33 Capri, for one
34 Rogers and Bean
35 Quatrain pattern
36 Circuit
37 Turned around
41 Edged, in a way
43 Assistance
46 To begin with
50 Hawaiian carving
53 Spoil
54 Knocking engine sounds
56 No __ roses (unenviable)
57 Outmatches
58 *Vera __* (Cooper film)
59 Aer Lingus land
60 Zero
62 Tropical nut
65 Fernando's aunt
66 Roscoe

8 EXPLETIVES DILUTED?

by Helen J. Stockton

ACROSS

1 Composer Khachaturian
5 Strikebreaker
9 Cell suffix
14 Joe Hardy's tempter
15 __ avail (useless)
16 Insignificant
17 FOR CRYING OUT LOUD
19 Nighttime noise
20 Greek monument
21 Hiding place
23 Kane's last thought
24 Get ready to rave
26 Two-wheeler of a sort
28 Enforcement power
30 Alternate
33 Predicament
36 Uproarious fellow
38 Like a lot
39 Onassis, for short
40 NUTS
42 Animation frame
43 Main street, in Milan
45 American bulrush
46 Card game for three
47 "Big deal!"
49 Dry and crumbly
51 Choreographer Alvin
53 Pinches
56 Orange-juice element
58 PBS show
60 Cop __
62 Mr. Detoo
64 RATS
66 Get ready to drive
67 Chow
68 Sleep __ (consider something overnight)
69 Western writer
70 Deadly sin
71 Hernando's hand

DOWN

1 Church garments
2 Runaway wins
3 Formal avenue
4 Vibraphonist's need
5 Pou __ (place to stand)
6 One of the brass
7 Part of AD
8 Intimate
9 Afts.
10 Paint oil
11 DARN IT
12 Miffed
13 '60s sitcom star
18 Have no use for
22 Ends a bout early
25 Queen of heaven
27 Spherical side dish
29 Tiresome
31 Scope
32 Shoe strip
33 Brits' raincoats
34 End for switch
35 GREAT SCOTT
37 Puts on the air
40 Diamond's ancestry
41 Durability
44 Leave port
46 Sneezing, for example
48 Finger count
50 Tale teller
52 Refrain from the mountains
54 General assemblies
55 Canary kin
56 Trodden way
57 Fertilizer chemical
59 French veal
61 Concerning
63 Unfold, in poesy
65 Superlative indicator

9 GOING UP

by Lee Weaver

ACROSS

1 "Put __ on it!"
5 Luxuriant, as vegetation
9 Not quite shut
13 Took the bus
14 See eye to eye
16 Large brass instrument
17 Angler's method
19 Certain government agents
20 Light lunches
21 Grumbled
23 Dove's sound
24 Egypt's continent
26 Breakfast breads
29 Trees native to 24 Across
31 Etcher's chemicals
32 Dirties
33 Halloween mo.
35 Gun the engine
36 Surly person
37 "Chances __" (Mathis tune)
38 Before, to Shelley
39 April forecasts
40 Binge
42 Moped
44 Encircled
45 Lazy ones
46 Wind direction: Abbr.
47 Invisible
49 Say over again
53 Professional charges
54 Emulate ivy
58 Cereal grains
59 Weird
60 Rough file
61 Greek portico
62 Old Russian ruler
63 Son of Seth

DOWN

1 Comments from Sandy
2 *Damn Yankees* role
3 Pastoral poem
4 Marred
5 Rodeo ropes
6 "Yuck!"
7 __ Lanka
8 Farm female
9 Region of ancient Greece
10 Join in an activity
11 Busy as __
12 McNally's map partner
15 Chinese appetizer
18 Graven images
22 Barbecue offerings
24 Teems
25 County festivals
26 Uncovered
27 Very tart
28 Engender
30 Mountainside erosion
32 More bashful
34 Irate, with "off"
36 Rhythmic speech
39 Part in a play
40 Tendon
41 Get ready
43 Ukrainian city
44 Baby-food name
47 Sci-fi vehicles
48 In apple-pie order
50 Pizazz
51 Furthermore
52 Recipe measurements: Abbr.
55 Allow
56 Tax org.
57 "Mamma __!"

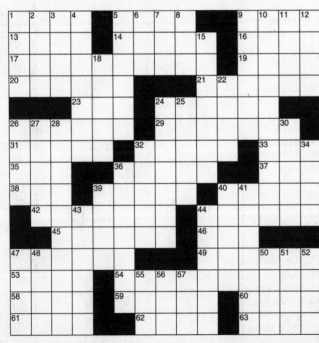

ACROSS

1 Spaghetti or linguini
6 African nation
10 Diamond call
14 Fuel carrier
15 Bard's river
16 Unfriendly dogs
17 Conscription group
19 Mine entrance
20 Actress Myrna
21 Do over, as a manuscript
23 Chat
27 Number One Son's surname
28 Important time
29 Baseball great Cobb et al.
30 Fall behind
31 First name in courtroom fiction
33 Russia's __ Mountains
37 All done
39 Gave up
40 Colorless
41 Trait carrier
42 On the briny
43 Ode title opening
44 Actress Ullmann
46 Mach 2 flier: Abbr.
48 See the sights
49 Omen
54 Like some cars, colorwise
55 Actor Beatty
56 Roof overhang
57 Football Hall of Fame rusher
63 __ Cong
64 Grocery-list element
65 Football's British relative
66 Word form for "within"
67 Indicates assent
68 Go bad

DOWN

1 Pea place
2 Televise
3 Patty Hearst's kidnappers: Abbr.
4 Nonstick stuff
5 __ Detoo
6 Nixon met him in China
7 Actress Gardner
8 Mr. Moto portrayer
9 Obliged
10 Obtains with effort
11 War hero Murphy
12 On the __ (broken)
13 First name in cosmetics
18 Computer data unit
22 Ironic
23 Use a razor
24 Tony-winner Uta
25 Joyce Kilmer poem
26 Most difficult
27 Plumbing problem
32 Hound holder
34 Point a finger at
35 Viva voce
36 Shakespearean king
38 Have a bearing on
39 Collapsing
45 __ Jima
47 Change for a fifty
48 Neaten
49 Actor McQueen
50 Huck Finn's creator
51 Wandered
52 "Cool!"
53 Has on
58 Took charge of
59 Printer's measures
60 Identity
61 Slugger's stat: Abbr.
62 Word segment: Abbr.

CHEEZIT!

by W.A. Hendricks

ACROSS

1 Mattress filling
6 La __ Tar Pits
10 Buster Brown's dog
14 "__ the Body Electric"
15 Group pronoun
16 Lupino and Tarbell
17 Wambaugh police book
20 Lid attachment
21 Neckline type
22 Silvers' sergeant
23 Nasal signal
25 Quaker pronoun
27 Get a mortgage
30 Factory closing
34 Liqueur flavoring
35 *Lion King* baddie
36 __-Magnon man
37 Murphy police movie
41 Summer, in Paris
42 Rifles and such
43 Severe
44 Loverboy
47 Earthy colors
48 Alan of *M*A*S*H*
49 Metrical message
50 Little dog
53 "Without a doubt!"
54 "__ sow, so shall . . ."
58 Travanti police show
62 Model Macpherson
63 Attractive guy
64 Sky-holding Titan
65 A bit too interested
66 __ Major
67 Sky blue

DOWN

1 Veto
2 Land east of the Urals
3 Defeats a wrestler
4 Tiny, as a town
5 Metric wts.
6 Embarrassing error
7 Uncouth
8 Verbal fill-ins
9 Hardwood tree
10 Neatened
11 Admired one
12 Stare awkwardly
13 Exxon, formerly
18 Declare
19 Encourage a crook
24 Person of action
25 Bangkok citizens
26 Fling forcefully
27 Noisy scene
28 __ a customer
29 Hard hat's fastener
30 Jerk
31 Come to pass
32 Inscribed
33 Slangy turndowns
35 Mideastern land
38 Frying fat
39 Spike the punch
40 Excessive sentimentality
45 British astronomer
46 Heidi's home
47 East, in Amsterdam
49 "__-boo!"
50 "Stop pouring!"
51 Hawaiian port
52 Sink joints
53 Itches
55 *Star Trek* officer
56 Fiscal period
57 In __ (actually)
59 Calendar abbr.
60 Capek play
61 Ewe sound

by Fred Piscop

ACROSS

1 Loose-limbed
6 Noggin
10 Pedestal topper
14 Fake drake
15 Bakery fixture
16 BMW rival
17 Dealer's declaration
19 Water conduit
20 __ carte
21 Chess-playing computer
23 Be a Nosy Parker
26 Chapter in history
27 Dash units
28 Single
31 Pants, slangily
33 Exiled Amin
34 Clinch, as a deal
36 Cultural character
39 Fontanne's partner
41 Orator Chauncey
43 Brewer's grain
44 Rink feints
46 Kindled anew
48 Diminutive suffix
49 Midmonth day
51 Haile __
53 Temple athlete
55 Hit broadside
57 Groove maker
58 El __ (Central American nation)
61 City on the Danube
62 Straight as __
63 Gobbledygook

68 *Daily Planet* reporter
69 Part of HOMES
70 Brownish photo tint
71 Jason's vessel
72 Tear apart
73 Senator Lott

DOWN

1 Say further
2 "That's amazing!"
3 Post-ER place
4 Pinpoint
5 Peeper protectors
6 Big name in chemicals
7 *The Art of Love* poet
8 Free-for-all
9 Finales
10 Poet's foot
11 Feature of some cars
12 Intense dislike
13 Come-ons
18 Tended to icy roads
22 Ashy
23 Weightlifter's concern
24 Excessive
25 Infield coup, slangily
29 Fancy pitcher
30 Suckers in
32 $$ dispenser
35 Soccer legend
37 Tie-twiddling comedian
38 Direct

40 Koppel or Knight
42 Done on purpose
45 Inmmunization fluids
47 Adjective for Everest
50 More bummed
52 Civil War fort
53 Honshu port
54 Heron or egret
56 *Arthur* star
59 Governor's prerogative
60 Lay waste to
64 Part of B&B
65 Tailless simian
66 Author Yutang
67 *Krazy __*

13 GRID WORK

by A.J. Santora

ACROSS
1 Relish ingredient
7 Sci. of farming
10 Diner order
13 Charm
14 Sporting weapon
15 Author Buscaglia
16 They avoid responsibility
18 Motor City org.
19 Request
20 Art medium
21 Emulate Thomas Crown
23 For fear that
25 Cartoon bird
27 Cardinal point
29 Top
30 Mini
33 USPS initials
34 Joan Cusack, to John
37 Court appointments
42 Paid spots
43 Oaxaca waterway
44 Hem in
45 Relaxes
48 Pass over
50 *Bonanza* actor
53 Game-show prize
57 Colt .45s, today
58 Vein contents
60 Altar constellation
61 Golf-club part
62 Memorable First Gulf War reporter
65 Chemical suffix
66 Needle case
67 Coin
68 __ Moines, IA
69 Filmdom's first King of Siam
70 Predicaments

DOWN
1 Conspiracy
2 Divert
3 Hockey items
4 Moose kin
5 Bank takeback
6 Flights
7 Barbary beast
8 Hamlet's mother
9 Close again
10 Prigs
11 Permission
12 High spot
14 Weather satellite
17 Job opening
22 Wabash st.
24 Have effect
26 Remove, as a hat
28 *Aladdin* prince
30 Hot spring
31 Pie ingredient
32 No-shows
33 Classic car
35 Fury
36 Aerospatiale product
38 Wood preservative
39 Word before brake or camera
40 Hoop group
41 Minimal progress, so to speak
46 What the *OED* isn't
47 Largo, vis-à-vis larghetto
48 Eastern European
49 Early bout
50 Saw
51 All together
52 Boutros' successor
54 Brings down the house
55 Goddess of peace
56 Car dealer's stock
59 Trig function
63 Illumination unit
64 Den sets

ACROSS

1 Air pollution
5 Cycle part
10 Canned meat
14 Floor covering, for short
15 Large church
16 Can't stand
17 Slangy suffix
18 Actress Angelina
19 Foul-smelling
20 Verbomaniac's fun
22 Nightclub
23 Mary's pet
24 Ireland's nickname
25 Underwater swimmer's gear
27 Purple shade
31 Jedi's power
32 Lawn cutter
33 Sunbeam
34 Chesspiece
35 La Scala site
36 Mrs. Copperfield
37 Aliens, for short
38 Before its time
39 Macho types
40 Gists
42 Passé
43 Like some hair
44 Patriot Nathan
45 Magnificence
47 "Jumbo shrimp," etc.
52 Jazzman Hines
53 Companions, casually
54 Gunk
55 "Shave __ haircut . . ."

56 Singer/guitarist from Spain
57 Poet Pound
58 Make a grating sound
59 __ time (use credit)
60 Size of writing paper

DOWN

1 Vast amount
2 Painter Joan
3 __ about (approximately)
4 "Break a leg!"
5 __ party (teen sleepover)
6 Nuclear weapon
7 Up to it
8 Six, in Seville
9 Cyclone center

10 Sure thing
11 "Never odd or even" is one
12 Working hard
13 Ancient Persian
21 Comic Kaplan
22 Brother, to Uncle Remus
24 Tied
25 Gets dirty in the chimney
26 Newspaper treats since 1913
27 Does nothing
28 On the road
29 Golden-__ corn
30 Tatum O'Neal's dad
31 At no cost
32 Entangle

35 Department-store founder
36 Cleansed
38 Begrudge
39 Angel topper
41 Cap attachment
42 Type of plum
44 Word form for "water"
45 Equipment
46 Actress Turner
47 Hawaiian island
48 Fracture photo
49 Slime
50 *Cheers* character
51 Alter
53 Toxic compound: Abbr.

15 SWEETHEARTS' DINNER

by Rich Norris

ACROSS
1 Chicken or turkey
5 Pocatello's state
10 Hayfield sight
14 Letters on a cross
15 Chinese cuisine
16 Like eager beavers
17 Attempt
18 Copycats
19 Supreme Greek deity
20 APPETIZER
23 Bald bird
24 Larry, Moe, and Curly
27 Fashion monogram
28 DEA employee
32 Trapshooting
33 Sorbonne summer
34 War-ending agreement
37 "Rule Britannia" composer
38 MAIN COURSE
40 "Puppy Love" singer
43 African expanse
44 Kimono sash
47 Unearthly
49 Wide-spouted pitcher
50 __ de plume
51 Courtroom figures
54 Prevent, to 51 Across
56 DESSERT
60 Bringer of bad luck
62 Quartet member
63 Lacking moisture
64 *Garfield* pooch
65 Lawn trimmer
66 Nonet number
67 Low in pitch
68 Construction toys
69 Clothes

DOWN
1 Suspicious look
2 How tuna may be ordered
3 Round up, as cattle
4 Slander relative
5 "If __ a Hammer"
6 Gullible one
7 From the start
8 Does damage to
9 Early stage
10 Antitank weapons
11 Mrs. Peel, for one
12 Brooklyn campus: Abbr.
13 Magazine VIPs
21 Meddlesome type
22 __ Alamos, NM
25 Yet, in poems
26 Sault __ Marie, MI
29 Jacket parts
30 First name in country music
31 Hidden stock
35 Defrost
36 Time past
38 Vocal-cord locales
39 Reduced, with "down"
40 Leatherworker's tool
41 Teachers' grp.
42 Service club since 1915
44 Michigan neighbor
45 Scheduled performance
46 Gets in the way of
48 Ph.D., e.g.
52 Take great pleasure (in)
53 Hit the dirt, in baseball
55 Barely sufficient
57 Verne's circumnavigator
58 Toast topping
59 Rowing-team members
60 Function
61 Author Tarbell

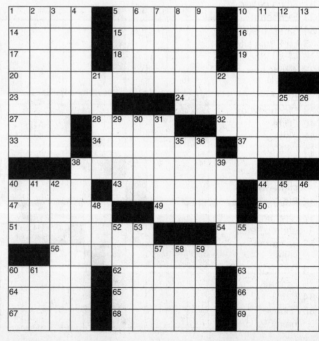

16 GREAT ESCAPES

by Patrick Jordan

ACROSS

1 Dubliner's dish
5 Gym floor pads
9 Hypnotist's command
14 Affectionate attention
15 Director Kazan
16 Pan or Piper
17 Away from the salty spray
18 46 Down resident
19 Polo's home
20 Escape artist's challenge
23 Input
24 Wraps completely around
28 One of Columbus' fleet
31 Draw out
32 Escape artist's challenge
37 Rush of floodwater
38 "Evil Woman" rock group
39 Adorn with droplets
41 Mauna __
42 Cake serving
45 Escape artist's challenge
48 High-ranking angel
50 Legacy recipient
51 Microscope component
54 Some inert elements
58 Escape artist's challenge
61 Basil-based sauce
64 Concept
65 Rent, as a limo
66 James __ Garfield
67 Cheek by jowl
68 Issue forth
69 27 Down type
70 Flubs one
71 Tarzan's neighbors

DOWN

1 Map need
2 Hawk's hook
3 Standing straight
4 Work respite
5 Pinochle action
6 Baldwin of film
7 Tenth part
8 "Old Scratch"
9 Rubylike gems
10 Reveal by accident
11 Greek vowel
12 Slim swimmer
13 Act the snoop
21 1980 Olympics hero Heiden
22 "__ Gotta Be Me"
25 Florida city
26 Mountaineer's support
27 Butcher-shop buy
29 Small protrusion
30 __ *Good Men*
32 *Steppenwolf* author
33 *Look Who's Talking* actress
34 Bête __
35 Org. that okays new medicines
36 Adam and Eve's youngest
40 Tiny
43 Rotating spindle
44 Embodiment
46 European capital
47 Windpipe
49 That lady
52 Queeg's ship
53 Downy duck
55 Underspend
56 Like ghost stories
57 Undoes a dele
59 Saline drop
60 Startles
61 Butter square
62 Recede
63 Sign at a hit B'way show

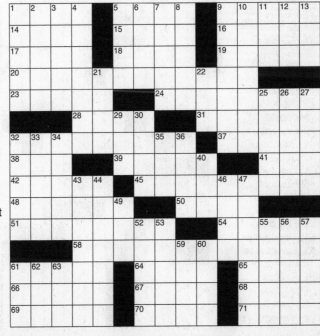

17 ON THE ROAD AGAIN
by Bob Lubbers

ACROSS
1 Writer LeShan
4 Make a raised seal
10 Shove
14 Instant lawn
15 Trail shelter
16 Archer or Meara
17 Highway interchange
19 From a distance
20 Eagle haven
21 Poet Teasdale
22 Music genre
23 Medical ritual
24 Most wan
26 Belgian resort
28 Road turn
29 Word form for "same"
30 Dine at home
32 Actress Shire
34 Agree
35 Marked walkway
38 Sirs' counterparts
39 Piedmont capital
40 Oceanfront
41 Palmer peg
42 Southern constellation
45 Nunn of Georgia
46 Disney duck
50 Pod pals
51 18-wheeler
53 Green moth
54 Plaster of __
55 Evening, to *Variety*
56 Place for non-speeders

58 Columnist Herb
59 Darkroom powder
60 Vietnamese New Year
61 Greek peak
62 Eubie Blake collaborator
63 Ames et al.

DOWN
1 Bust out
2 They mete
3 Worships
4 Gen. Robt. __
5 French sea
6 Type of vinegar
7 *Peyton Place* star
8 Gawk
9 Settees

10 Carson's predecessor
11 Detach
12 Turtle activity
13 Part of HRH
18 Red-carpet treader
24 Actress Negri et al.
25 Actress O'Shea
27 Tiny colonist
29 Hurt
31 "It's __ to Tell a Lie"
32 Mount Snow lift
33 1998 Tony-winning play
34 __ as a beet
35 Babe Didrikson __
36 Esau's descendants

37 Remote provinces
38 Writers' submissions: Abbr.
42 Treat with gas
43 Poured
44 One's holdings
47 Korbut's namesakes
48 "The Flying Finn"
49 Writer Nin
50 Sidekick
52 Actress Rowlands
54 WWII journalist
55 Cpl., e.g.
57 Lon __ of Cambodia

18 TRUMP TOWERS

by Manny Nosowsky

ACROSS

1 Stop up
5 Nickname for a free spender
15 Late-night name
16 Spiritual goal
17 Golden Rule word
18 Like some questions
19 Ruhr road
20 Latest word
21 Cabbage
22 *Evita* character
23 Doctor's drug bk.
24 Role for Barbra
26 Inn place
28 Dog-paddled
30 Out of control
31 Ustinov Oscar film
36 European intro
37 Tale of Troy
38 With a pin, it's a lock
39 Recited easily
41 Hines' nickname
42 Snorkeling site
43 Pushed sideways, as text
44 Cabaret cousins
47 CPO's outfit
48 "All the Things You __"
49 Heavy hammer
50 Bruhn of ballet
52 Went quickly by
53 Honeyed word
56 Actor Ray
57 Sensitive topics
58 Roulette bet
59 "__ Hotel" (Elvis tune)
60 Messy stuff

DOWN

1 Heavily upholstered furniture
2 Witch in *The Wiz*
3 Supplementally
4 Thug
5 Fräulein's frock
6 ". . . robins __ hair"
7 In a different form
8 New York team
9 Coronado's quest
10 *All Things Considered* network
11 Lower oneself
12 Lies: Lat.
13 Poker challenge
14 Go soft
23 Favorite
24 Swing place
25 CPR pro
27 Cat's-paw
28 __ up (improve the look of)
29 British flyer's support group of WWII
31 Gin flavoring
32 Jezebel's husband
33 '65 role for Jane Fonda
34 Introduced
35 Data gathering, perhaps
37 March time
40 Afore
41 Aficionado
43 "My, oh my!"
44 Human-powered vessel
45 Actress Lindley
46 One on the run
47 Utah's __ Mountains
49 Woven fabric
50 Sheik colleague
51 Philosopher Descartes
52 Tooth of a sort
54 Bldg. unit
55 Lowe or Reiner

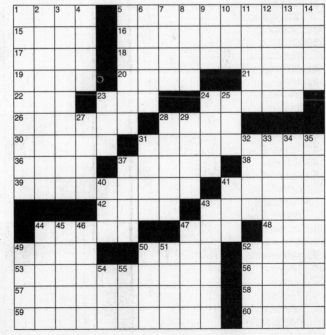

by W.A. Hendricks

ACROSS
1 Gait
5 Wide tie
10 Downhill racer
14 __ call on (visit)
15 Abraham's wife
16 Ocean motion
17 Cake finisher
18 Comical bandleader Jones
19 Book leaf
20 "Forget it!"
22 Whodunit revelation
24 "__ it my way"
26 Actor M. __ Walsh
27 Kitten's quality
30 Spotted cat
34 Stopovers
35 Unruffled
37 Maine town
38 Compete
39 Showing favoritism
41 Crow sound
42 "__ Easy" (Ronstadt song)
44 Musical work
45 Related
46 "__ vie!"
48 Fan club
50 Map collection
52 Lose traction
53 Whodunit roster
56 Pound and Stone
59 Milky gem
60 Sharon of Israel
63 Football shutout line score

64 Finished
65 Showy flower
66 Something prohibited
67 R __ (time off)
68 British coins
69 Prayer ender

DOWN
1 Revolve
2 Tex-Mex treat
3 Whodunit interrogatee
4 Public processions
5 Stubborn equine
6 Tree output
7 Tony Perkins movie of 1984
8 Caulking material

9 Word form for "hot"
10 Noted gatekeeper
11 Truth bender
12 Precipice
13 Forest creature
21 Yang's partner
23 Ornamentation
25 Art __
27 Urban
28 Get together
29 Hernando de __
31 Whodunit location, perhaps
32 Walking __ (happy)
33 Hamlets
36 Acclaim

39 Actor Nick
40 Dogmas
43 Office item
45 Flagstaff's state
47 Fearless Fosdick creator
49 DDE, to friends
51 "...a poem lovely as __"
53 Carbonated drink
54 "Once __ a time..."
55 Hourglass filler
57 Top-rated
58 Any day now
61 Business letter abbr.
62 Alkaline solution

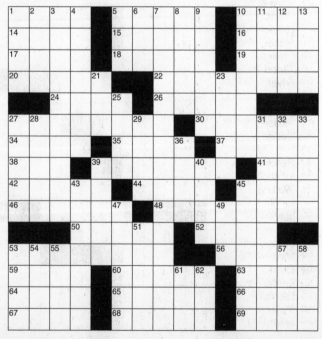

20 FALSE PROPHETS

by Rich Norris

ACROSS

1 Cries audibly
5 "Get lost!"
10 Former Iranian ruler
14 Citrus variety
15 Sum of the parts
16 Actress Hatcher
17 Elevator inventor
19 Position in the hierarchy
20 Buddhist sect
21 Els' followers
22 High home
23 Early 19th-century orator
28 Wine barrels
30 Roof overhangs
31 Western Indian
32 Made sounds while sleeping
34 Grand __ Opry
37 Unknown, as an author: Abbr.
38 Chair fixer
39 "Good buddy" driver
40 Pomeranian or parakeet
41 Picasso, for one
42 Not quite shut
43 :
44 Readies, for short
45 *Waiting for Godot* playwright
50 Like some college walls
51 Mine matter
52 Quick swim
55 Leslie Caron title role
56 *Mouse Hunt* actor
60 Former Fed-head Greenspan
61 Short
62 Johnson of *Laugh-In*
63 Did a number
64 Writer's rep
65 Move no more

DOWN

1 Mideast canal
2 Stare at
3 Rearview-mirror concern
4 Family nickname
5 Hindu honorific
6 Selected
7 Balderdash
8 One of the Babas
9 Month, in Madrid
10 Accentuate
11 Organ with chambers
12 Much-admired golfer
13 Boy Scout, at times
18 Farm females
22 All tucked in
24 Related
25 Like Simba
26 Hawker's merchandise
27 Chris of tennis
28 Bloke
29 First-rate
32 Racing boat
33 Influential individual
34 Curio
35 Jump high
36 Goes awry
39 Dessert vehicle
41 Like most colleges
43 Helping from offstage, perhaps
44 Hammer part
45 __ *Marner*
46 City near Madrid
47 Italian city
48 Songwriter Leonard
49 Borden competitor
53 Fascinated by
54 Slightest sound
56 Celtics' org.
57 S. Amer. country
58 Overtime cause
59 __ Cruces, NM

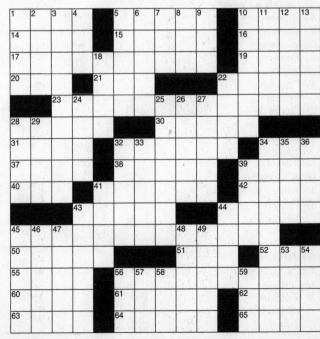

21 THANKSGIVING FEAST

by Lee Weaver

ACROSS
1 Coat-collar fold
6 Western plateau
10 Short snooze
13 Musical dramas
15 In excess of
16 Bikini part
17 Hot-dog topper
18 Pays no attention to
20 Star's backstage quarters
22 Creme cookie
23 Capri or Wright
27 Wild guess
31 Get down to business
35 Created a basket
36 Soothsayer
37 __ Got a Secret
38 Archaeological period
42 Well-bred
44 Modern
45 Tide type
47 Coat-of-arms border
48 Sinecure
52 Furtive whisper
53 Ford's *Star Wars* role
54 Part of
56 Is extraordinary
64 Parting word
67 One who hazards a view
68 Genetics letters
69 Canal to Buffalo
70 Ramble
71 Addams Family cousin
72 Low cart

73 Sudden transitions

DOWN
1 Nobleman
2 Imitator
3 Soccer great
4 Goddess of discord
5 Rodeo rope
6 Genghis Khan's followers
7 At any time
8 Western lily
9 Folk singer Guthrie
10 Network owned by GE
11 Craft or skill
12 __ de deux
14 Upper garment
19 Kuwaiti ruler

21 Teacher's org.
24 Aspen visitors
25 Carpenters' tools
26 Hole in one's shoe
27 Playground equipment
28 Matador, e.g.
29 Affirmation
30 Jerry's partner
32 Beer barrel
33 Golf gadget
34 Coffee server
39 Unspecified amount
40 Obtain
41 Corn unit
43 See 14 Down
46 Tie pattern
49 Cast a ballot

50 Bankbook abbr.
51 Emphatic refusal
55 Asian kingdom
57 Profoundly impressed
58 *From Here to Eternity* actress
59 Lamb's pen name
60 Film, in France
61 ". . . a bushel __ peck"
62 Don't give up
63 Makes mistakes
64 Part of TGIF
65 Powerful insect
66 Squealer

22 KEYED UP

by Brendan Quigley

ACROSS

1 Sonic the Hedgehog maker
5 Baja houses
10 Drop of gel
13 "I smell __!"
14 Elroy's pet
15 Masters shout
16 12 to 8
18 Deal preceder
19 Desalinization input
20 Devious maneuvers
21 Congregation affirmation
22 Prepared to be knighted
24 Cat, at times
27 Act of respect
30 Is next to
31 Do damage to
32 Aware of
33 "Smoking or __?"
34 Nickname for Ruth
37 Shooting marble
38 Small job to do
40 Actress Lena
41 Reside
43 Action-film crew
45 Simpers
46 Role for Madonna
47 Word of encouragement
48 Soft and crumbly
50 Chinese city
54 Part of UPI

55 Forster novel
57 RR stops
58 Clock partner
59 *"Dies __"*
60 Cry
61 Shell competitor
62 "Bye!"

DOWN

1 Without
2 Part of HOMES
3 Dotty
4 Transversely
5 Furniture wheel
6 Pale
7 Use a swizzle stick
8 Dog sound
9 Barfly

10 Warning sign
11 Pretentious
12 "The __ knees"
15 Become the job of
17 Least wild
20 According to
22 Sacred text of Islam
23 Unfeeling
24 Is winded
25 WWII vessel
26 Drinks on credit
27 Pioneer's place
28 Follow closely
29 Mournful cries
31 Paris abductee

35 __ sapiens
36 Cards expert Hoyle
39 Bell sounds
42 Improvises
44 Adjudicate
45 Hypocritically earnest
47 Nautical reference
48 Hit's partner
49 Word form for "within"
50 Heavy blow
51 Zeus' sister
52 Med. school course
53 Brainchild
55 Witch, to Shakespeare
56 Bullring cry

23 CAT-O'-NINE-TAILS

by Fred Piscop

ACROSS

1 "Woe is me!"
5 Brother of Adam
9 Prepare to drive
14 Campaign '96 name
15 Greek letter
16 Sheeplike
17 French romantic painter
19 One of the Gabors
20 Pundits
21 Amscrayed
23 Dog-days forecast
24 Law
26 In need of a map
28 TV's Nick at __
29 Syracuse, NY, college
32 Pea-souper
35 Wielded an épée
37 Siberia's continent
38 Orderly grouping
40 Yuletide quaff
41 Dumped out
42 Honest-to-goodness
43 Personnel paper
45 Simple signatures
46 Nessie, for one
48 Grindery
50 Stags' mates
51 Indochine actress
54 Gillespie's music
56 Milky Way unit
58 Not alfresco
60 Everglades wader
62 Obsolete printer type
64 Tot's transport
65 Highly rated
66 Novel ending
67 Put the whammy on
68 Circus barker
69 Actor Tamblyn

DOWN

1 Tacks on
2 Erstwhile theater chain
3 __ once (suddenly)
4 Naval rank
5 Hairy
6 Hugs, symbolically
7 Steps over a fence
8 __-Coburg-Gotha
9 Powwow percussion
10 Stowe character
11 Toss out
12 Word-processor command
13 Bog stuff
18 Make urban
22 Got out of town
25 Sawbuck
27 Motel freebie
29 Lentil, for one
30 Aswan Dam river
31 Vittles
32 Woodstock setting
33 Layered cookie
34 International road race
36 NYSE listings
39 To boot
41 Jennifer Lopez role
43 Take a break
44 Barely adequate
47 Did lab work
49 Sheen
51 Bagpipe sound
52 Love of fine art
53 Blue-pencils
54 Sister of Meg
55 Folklore fiend
57 Commotions
59 Former mates
61 __ out a living
63 It's bagged at the supermarket

24 UP A TREE

by Lee Weaver

ACROSS

1 Send, as a parcel
5 Musical postscript
9 Explosive letters
12 Wastelands
14 Airline to Israel
15 Big name in supercomputers
16 Vulnerable
18 Lie in wait
19 A+ and C–
20 Abundant wealth
22 Fresh talk
24 A+ and C–
25 Maglie or Mineo
28 Actress Winslet
30 Farming ground
31 High cards
33 Levin and Gershwin
35 Jules Verne's genre
38 "I smell __!"
39 Keeps at it
41 Soon, poetically
42 Put back on the skillet
44 Slangy affirmative
45 Main role
46 Make airtight
48 Make a sketch
50 Foxy
51 Bowler's pickup
52 Card game
54 Italian cheese
57 Throws out
61 Theater award
62 Calculator button
64 Tear apart
65 On the __ (estranged)
66 Rodeo rope
67 Energy unit
68 Space shuttle grp.
69 Weaver's reed

DOWN

1 Dirty air
2 Little-hand indication
3 Tiny amount
4 Urges on
5 Animation frame
6 Hodgepodge
7 Somewhat moist
8 Places for photos
9 Major phone connections
10 Antidrug agents
11 Little kid
13 Go furtively
15 Like some office jobs
17 Attack vigorously
21 Neighbor of Thailand
23 Wander off
25 Rhineland region
26 Ranch unit
27 Auto-suspension part
29 Alleviated
32 Flowed copiously
34 Telescope sights
36 Infant Appaloosa
37 __ 500 (auto race)
40 Salt dispenser
43 Maneuverable, as a yacht
47 Teaching session
49 Be unable to decide
51 Cavalry sword
53 Grows weary
54 Skin opening
55 Light greenish-blue
56 Pistachios, e.g.
58 Fossil fuel
59 Sizable purse
60 Command to Rover
63 Flat __ pancake

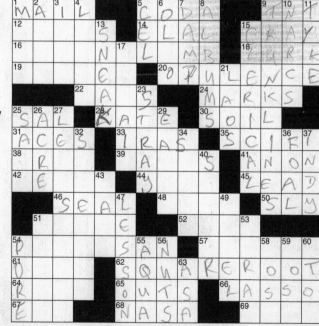

25 WE'RE NOT DRESSING

by Fred Piscop

ACROSS

1 Ending for hippo- or aero-
6 Tree fluids
10 Yellowstone beast
14 De Valera of Ireland
15 Matador's foe
16 Egg on
17 First course with a cheese topping
20 Watch over
21 Novelist Waugh
22 Burros
23 Tummy trouble
25 Beat by a whisker
27 Cool confection
31 Not quite dry
35 "When pigs fly!"
36 Ponder, with "over"
38 SSE, e.g.
39 Fr. holy woman
40 __ stone (hieroglyphics key)
43 Wyo. neighbor
44 Drop the ball
45 Home Depot rival
46 Grab the tab
48 "Cheerio!"
50 Cattleman's abode
53 Authentic
55 Regretted
56 Internet posting
59 Aid in a felony
61 Nerd
65 High-risk game
68 __ Jury (Spillane novel)
69 Ground grain
70 Fit to be tied
71 Steinway's ivories
72 Understanding response
73 German industrial city

DOWN

1 Nimble-fingered
2 Seldom seen
3 Foreboding sign
4 Carter's vice president
5 SASE, e.g.
6 Like a fence's wares
7 Tiptop
8 Retailer's ploy
9 Jack of *Barney Miller*
10 Gave a smooch to
11 Greek love god
12 Flu symptom
13 Sales agents
18 "That's hilarious!"
19 Over-the-hill horse
24 Wispy clouds
26 Shoulder muscle, briefly
27 Map detail
28 Aquarium fish
29 Ward off
30 "That is . . ."
32 Toulouse "Toodle-oo"
33 Exemplar of greed
34 Ramble on
37 Turning tool
41 Gumbo veggie
42 Shipping routes
47 Composer of *Oklahoma!*
49 Crops up
51 New Orleans cuisine
52 Rwandan ethnic group
54 Ingenious Whitney
56 Composer Satie
57 Trumpeter's doodad
58 Very pale
60 Scottish hillside
62 JFK postings
63 Diminutive ending
64 Sharp as a tack
66 "What __, chopped liver?"
67 Tell a whopper

26 NATURALIST AUTHORS

by Rich Norris

ACROSS

1. Chinese ships
6. Quietly understood
11. Bowie or Brady
14. Bridge bid, for short
15. Islam's God
16. Yoko __
17. *The Agony and the Ecstasy* author
19. *Id* __
20. Nifty
21. At the summit
22. Convenience store
24. Actor Danson
25. CIA employee
26. Throne covering
28. Cut drastically, as prices
30. Baseball stat
32. *The Ghost and Mrs.* __
33. Tested in class
36. Helps out
37. *The Tin Drum* author
39. *Leaving Las Vegas* actress
41. Rubber products
42. Seep
43. Wks. and wks.
44. Like many kids' rooms
48. Takeout favorites
50. Crucial
52. However, briefly
53. Vehicle with runners
54. __' Pea (*Popeye* kid)
56. Small songbird
57. Had dinner
58. *All This and Heaven Too* author

61. Yonder damsel
62. Hi-tech communication
63. Actor Guttenberg
64. Sponsor's spots
65. Contemptible
66. Speak

DOWN

1. Knees and knuckles
2. Disentangle, as fishing line
3. The Sagebrush State
4. Work with yarn
5. Peter, to Henry
6. Scrumptious
7. Sax range
8. Horse-on-pavement sound
9. Author Fleming
10. Bara of silents
11. '40s heavyweight champ
12. Tasteless
13. Bon __ (witticism)
18. Wide opening
23. As a group
25. Avoid
26. Military training group
27. Multiples of 43 Across
29. Extract juice
30. Poet Pound et al.
31. Rules of conduct, for short
34. News bits
35. Goose egg
37. Gas __ (inefficient cars)

38. Troop group
39. Absorb, with "up"
40. Lifted up
45. Thoroughfare
46. Put away, for now
47. Thataway
49. Pertinent, in Latin
50. Jazz singer Smith
51. Sniggler's quarry
54. Examine in detail
55. Tory rival
56. Skater from Germany
57. "Eureka!"
59. Doc's grp.
60. Seminoles' sch.

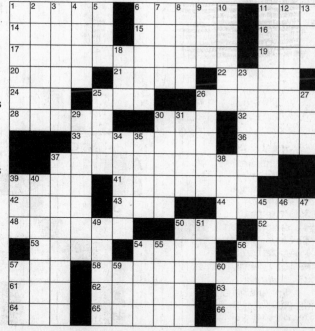

IN THE WAY

by Patrick Jordan

ACROSS

1 Hooded serpent
6 Comedian's stock
10 Thick piece
14 Portland Hoffa's hubby
15 Free-for-all
16 World's longest river
17 Reason for a street closing
19 Pot payment
20 German article
21 Camera part
22 Gilligan's Island feature
24 Skelton, e.g.
26 Vitality
27 "__ My Party"
28 Rude ones
32 Electrical units
35 Crave
36 Onetime wives
37 DeMille specialty
38 Hemispherical roofs
39 Ale measure
40 Well-heeled
41 Folksinger Burl
42 Gridlock components
43 Honeycombed homes
45 48 __ (Murphy movie)
46 Desktop trash can, for one
47 Astronomical distances
51 Online menace
54 Comical Curtin
55 X-ray supplement
56 California city
57 Certain folk performer
60 Have coming
61 Laid-back quality

62 *Touched by an Angel* star
63 Air resistance
64 Prepared Easter eggs
65 Keeps in the manuscript

DOWN

1 Pole tossed by Scots
2 Stan's chum
3 Redford, for one
4 VCR button
5 Short socks
6 Majestic
7 What snobs put on
8 Received
9 Salon staffers
10 Toon feline
11 Floor covering, for short
12 Chorus member
13 Existed
18 Rolling veggies
23 *A Bug's Life* character
25 Thumbing for rides
26 Sectors
28 Director Cameron
29 Walk offstage
30 Clinton's attorney general
31 Aircraft introduced in 1976
32 Trick or treat
33 Sheriff Andy's boy
34 Canine pests
35 Crafted on a loom

38 Like 36 Across
42 Overdue debts
44 Party purchase
45 Round of applause
47 Summoned, nowadays
48 Toastmaster
49 Colgate competitor
50 Begets
51 Weeded the garden
52 Not quite closed
53 Irene of *Fame* fame
54 Greco or Feliciano
58 Put down, as carpeting
59 Aerialist's insurance

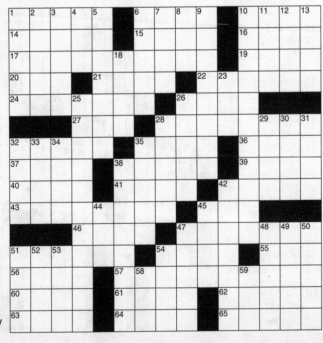

28 PASSING PARADE

by Bob Lubbers

ACROSS

1 Pat down
5 RAF flyer
9 Cons
14 Gen. Robt. __
15 Solidarity name
16 Worry
17 Hit the road
18 Curved molding
19 Scent
20 Motorist's sights of yesteryear
23 Spring mo.
24 React to yeast
25 Witch craft
29 Achiever
31 Hindu deity
35 Musket loader
37 The __ (Afrikaans)
39 Swell time
40 Motorist's sights of yesteryear
43 Barbie's beau
44 Achy
45 '20s English Channel swimmer
46 Actress Martinelli
48 Word form for "dry"
50 Tyne's family
51 "__ go bragh"
53 Usher's creator
55 Motorist's sight of yesteryear
63 Cowboy contest
64 "Vaya con __"

65 Russian river
66 Mr. T's bunch
67 Allay
68 Pro __
69 Horace and Thomas
70 Canonized *femmes*: Abbr.
71 __ off (angry)

DOWN

1 Hawaiian Isls., once
2 *Inter* __
3 Care beginning
4 Banana skin
5 Clumsy mistake
6 Look upon
7 On the rocks
8 Alexander epithet
9 They may be reserved
10 Life's work
11 Mite
12 *Auntie* __
13 Getz or Laurel
21 Actor Novarro et al.
22 Rickenbacker, for one
25 Shattered
26 "Bolero" composer
27 Harbingers
28 Hockey great
30 Catchall category
32 "I want __ just like . . ."
33 Macho

34 Dunderheads
36 Toxic compound
38 Path to success
41 Infantry weapons
42 Arthur or Lillie
47 Greek sea
49 Side against
52 Motel units
54 Sahara stops
55 Wee bit
56 Smidgen
57 City in Yemen
58 *South Pacific* child
59 Writer Vonnegut
60 "*Dies* __"
61 Hoopster Archibald
62 Pleased

by W.A. Hendricks

ACROSS

1 Charitable collection
5 Possessed
8 "__ Entertain You"
13 Chimney dirt
14 57 Across book
15 Multiple-choice choice
16 __ about (approximately)
17 Bates or Alda
18 Scarlett's spouse
19 57 Across book
22 Observe
23 Chicago trains
24 Common surname
26 *Wizard of Oz* character
31 Sequence
34 *Six Million Dollar Man* org.
35 "For Me and __"
37 Muscle power
38 Floor coverings
40 Long-plumed bird
42 Tract of wet ground
43 Nevada lake
45 Tabloid exclusive
47 Playful bite
48 Wedding spots
50 Precise
52 Part of Iberia
54 Former global carrier: Abbr.
55 Burnt residue
57 Subject of the puzzle
63 Singer Cleo
65 Change direction
66 Inventor's basis
67 Propose
68 Goes wrong
69 Bridge player's feat
70 Rose and Rozelle
71 __ down (massage)
72 In this place

DOWN

1 __ yet (so far)
2 Actress Anderson
3 Othello, e.g.
4 Thoroughfare
5 Hawaiian dance
6 Open a crack
7 Taboos
8 Trucks along the Thames
9 Ordinal ending
10 57 Across book
11 Parcel (out)
12 Art Deco name
14 Film based on stories by 57 Across
20 Meager
21 Typesetter's units
25 Quick haircut
26 Major blood vessel
27 Ordinary
28 57 Across story collection
29 Breakfast choice
30 Explorer Polo
32 Scary
33 Used a broom
36 Boxer Spinks
39 Daytime drama
41 Wobbles
44 Pencil toppers
46 Chesspiece
49 Watch the kids
51 Jaunty
53 Not even once
55 Unbalanced
56 Out of danger
58 Cuzco's country
59 Sage or basil
60 Inactive
61 Within arm's reach
62 Baseball or backgammon
64 Born: Fr.

by Bob Lubbers

ACROSS

1 *Moby-Dick* captain
5 Inventor Nikola
10 Pro __ (in proportion)
14 Tiresome one
15 Medieval helmet
16 Swelled heads
17 Blue-blood group
19 Whistle sound
20 SAT takers, e.g.
21 Italian entrée
23 Parcel of land
24 "Thank you, Pierre!"
25 Guys
28 "Merry" month
29 Vietnamese area
33 __ out a living
34 Russian space station
35 Jacket part
36 Undesired expansion
40 Bay windows
41 Guggenheim display
42 Day: Sp.
43 __ Fe, NM
44 Soissons summer
45 Interrogate
47 Writer Zola
49 Pub serving
50 In the wrong role
53 Most evenhanded
57 Landed
58 Pullman reservation
60 __-Japanese War
61 Poet's inspiration
62 "It's a Sin to Tell __"
63 Fortune-teller
64 Philosopher Kierkegaard
65 Bruce or Laura

DOWN

1 Place against
2 Aspiration
3 Some French paintings
4 Scarab
5 "Don't play," to a musician
6 Goofs
7 Dallas campus: Abbr.
8 Reporter Stahl
9 Perfume oil
10 Lawyer's fee
11 Eagerly excited
12 Roger Rabbit, for one
13 Movie terrier
18 Classic cars
22 Head part
24 British seaside resort
25 Office notes
26 Director Kurosawa
27 Ushered
28 Sara or Farrow
30 "__ say more?"
31 To no __ (useless)
32 Military award
34 French for "my"
35 Onetime Orly arr.
37 Mine __ (soldier's tool)
38 Guanaco kin
39 Before, to a poet
44 Corrida beast
45 Smooth-talking
46 Double-check copy
48 Small spots of land
49 Burr or Copland
50 Church service
51 Nastase of tennis
52 Trig function
53 Lavish party
54 First name in mystery
55 Agitate
56 At that time
59 Armed conflict

ACROSS

1 One of three squares
5 Spider's handiwork
8 One of Edison's 1000+
14 Perry's creator
15 Chopping tool
16 Flat sharer
17 Manitoba tribe
18 Badminton need
19 Director May
20 Creeping weed
23 Apothecary's weight
24 Even if, for short
25 Commercial alliances
27 Wilson of The Beach Boys
29 Web-toed mammal
33 Iraqi or Qatari
37 Tarzan's movie son
38 Ruling threesome
39 Part of some spares
41 Harry Connick Jr., for one
42 Film festival site
43 __ Lanka
44 Fill with cargo
45 Send to the capital
46 Aiming aid
48 Moses of filmdom
50 Untouchables, e.g.
55 Pull an all-nighter, perhaps
58 Any of the Ramones
60 Emissary of the pope
62 AFL's partner
63 Tart taste
64 Merle of *Wuthering Heights*
65 Zeta follower
66 Football legend Graham
67 Acted the valet
68 Sun Yat-__
69 Jay's home

DOWN

1 Hajji's destination
2 Flynn of film
3 Sitka dweller
4 Parasitic person
5 Word-processing pioneer
6 Backbreaking effort
7 Electron stream
8 Weight-room exercise
9 "You've got mail" co.
10 Inedible mushroom
11 Mideast bigwig
12 Actress Foch
13 Abound
21 Goblin starter
22 Catch some rays
26 Spanish zodiac animal
28 Grand-slam foursome
30 Rock singer Turner
31 Supplemented, with "out"
32 Seldom seen
33 Suffix with utter or suffer
34 100 dinars
35 One of the Brontës
36 Standard of excellence
38 Send sprawling
40 *Our Gang* dog
41 Rather's predecessor
43 Candle holders
46 Early Beatle Sutcliffe
47 Environment-alist's prefix
49 Pay out
51 Follow, as advice
52 Do figure eights
53 Circus setups
54 Grain bane
55 Filly's footfall
56 McEntire of country
57 Antiquing agent
59 Mottled horse
61 Wingtip tip

by Rich Norris

ACROSS

1 Crushed underfoot
5 Traffic tie-ups
9 Homebuyer's option
14 Inconsiderate
15 News item, briefly
16 *X-Files* extra
17 Cain's victim
18 Bear in the air
19 Alamo locale
20 Like a comedian
23 Tutoring unit
24 Significant period
25 Tina's ex
28 Fed. benefits grp.
29 Cutlet meat
32 Coin
34 Enters, as data
36 Jazzman Thelonious
37 Like a nitpicker
41 Shake up
42 Scented case
43 Behaves willfully
46 Fair grades
47 Two-time Tony winner Hagen
50 *King Kong* studio
51 __ Paulo
53 Carpentry machine
55 Physically demanding
58 Letterman forte
61 Space
62 Relationship phrase
63 Flawless concept
64 Landing place
65 Piggies, in a tot's rhyme
66 Flat agreement
67 "__ be a pleasure!"
68 Actor Griffith

DOWN

1 Fishing nets
2 Red stones
3 Ukrainian seaport
4 Removes
5 Long trips
6 Julie's *East of Eden* role
7 Catchall category: Abbr.
8 Tomato-plant support
9 Forty winks
10 First name in fashion
11 Squelch, as a proposal
12 Narc employer: Abbr.
13 Switch positions
21 Entertainment charge
22 April 15th grp.
25 Sacred image
26 Crowned checker
27 "A mouse!"
30 Egyptian cobras
31 New Hampshire state flower
33 Send out
34 Do-it-yourselfers' needs
35 Agreeable
37 Get a loan on
38 Choir member
39 Steinbeck story
40 Electrical inventor
41 Cookie holder
44 Suited for the purpose
45 Cal.'s ocean
47 Perfect accord
48 Protected, as an outdoor party
49 Large merchant ship
52 Giraffe relative
54 Watchdog breed
55 Prejudice
56 Chelsea chap
57 Film unit
58 Feel out of sorts
59 JFK predecessor
60 Rural expanse

33 MALE CALL

by Lee Weaver

ACROSS

1 Velvety lichen
5 Gives approval
12 Dime-a-dozen
14 Direct route
15 Bring to light
17 Less likely
18 Suffice
20 Mental impressions
21 Florence's river
22 Wooded valley
26 Sleek jets
27 Reproduction
28 Spooky
29 Signature
31 Captivate
35 __ Off (backstage farce)
36 British army private
40 Makes an effort
41 Sleep phases
42 Mascara target
46 Iowa State site
47 Fictional plantation
48 Fracas
49 Doohickey
51 Variety of apple
55 Pot marjoram
56 Cockamamie
57 Champagne glasses
58 Place for a play
59 Mrs. Dick Tracy

DOWN

1 Pennies or dollars
2 Denver or Spanish
3 Some shirts
4 Classifies
5 Licorice-flavored liqueur
6 String quartet member
7 Put in acoustical tile, perhaps
8 Shade tree
9 Lower
10 Point opposite WSW
11 Rev.'s address
12 Sleeve ends
13 Ultimate degree
16 '70s prime minister
19 Substance in cereals
22 Word form meaning "tenth"
23 Cupid
24 Tiny parasites
25 Albanian coins
27 Marsh bird
28 Baseball great Slaughter
29 Great pleasures
30 Miller and Richards
31 James of jazz
32 Rule of thumb
33 Georges' girlfriend
34 *Sras.*, across the Pyrenees
37 Ballclub employee
38 "I Won't Dance" composer
39 Adult insect
42 Sports group
43 Slugger's stat
44 Paving pieces
45 Wanderers of the road
47 Quaker pronoun
48 Process, as ore
49 Taunt
50 Doghouse sound
51 Flying mammal
52 Ember, later
53 First UN head
54 Chromosome part

34 WELL DONE

by Norma Steinberg

ACROSS
1 Mutt's pal
5 Zoo enclosure
9 Service-station purchase
12 Ventilated
14 Wooden peg
15 River: Sp.
16 Nostalgic time
18 Sprite
19 Tends to the lawn
20 Have stamina
21 Paid out
24 Believe appropriate
26 Apply, as with an atomizer
28 Study, with "on"
31 Milk: Fr.
32 Holler
35 __ acid
36 Supply with weapons
37 Least difficult
39 Bigwig, initially
40 Sirloin, e.g.
42 And others: Abbr.
43 Small bug
44 Animosity
46 Building fronts
48 Entomologist's subject
51 Intertwined
52 Ticklish doll
54 Ross of *Happy Days*
56 Commit perjury
57 Food emporium
62 Encountered
63 Vicinities
64 Go away
65 Part truck, part car: Abbr.
66 Dweeb
67 Recolored

DOWN
1 Binge
2 Vowel sequence
3 To and __
4 Gave dinner to
5 Encryptions
6 Conscious
7 Old Faithful, e.g.
8 Raised railways
9 Rocky Mountain watershed
10 Feels poorly
11 Cushy
13 Cushy
14 Banned insecticide
17 One of the Jacksons
20 Actor Neeson
21 Greek city-state
22 Evening viewing
23 Consume
25 Accomplishment
26 Cut, as prices
27 Race-winning margin, sometimes
29 Joined
30 Pius and Leo
33 Sense of humor
34 Page in a book
37 Supplements, with "out"
38 Ski race
41 Florentine river
43 Fleetwood __
45 Bashful
47 Erie or Suez
49 Antic
50 Tire part
52 Shade trees
53 Stead
55 April 15 addressee
57 __ Remo, Italy
58 Blushing
59 Jay follower
60 Second person in Genesis
61 Media mogul Turner

35 GETTING A WHUPPING

by Fred Piscop

ACROSS

1 Difficult journeys
6 Cleaning tool
9 Come apart at the seams
14 Actor Quinn
15 Have a bug
16 Atmospheric layer
17 Swimming stroke
19 Exemplar of greed
20 High-__ (one in the fast lane)
21 Hair-cream dollop
23 Take a load off
24 Church recesses
26 Hardly ever
28 Squares, vis-à-vis quadrilaterals
31 Salad choice
33 Forty-niner's find
34 Bleak, in verse
36 Mah-jongg units
39 Pickle pick
41 Seamen spin them
43 Old Italian cash
44 Fur-trading name
46 See-through
48 French diarist
49 Apply balm to
51 Word with cross- or bandy-
53 Cavort
55 Mongol invader
57 __ Tin Tin
58 *Krazy* __
60 Precious

64 Non-studio film, for short
66 Cyclonic storm
68 Star's rep
69 Proud __ peacock
70 Rival of Sealy and Simmons
71 Poetic times of day
72 Zodiac beast
73 Check for fit

DOWN

1 Young 'uns
2 Knee slapper
3 Upper hand
4 Greek letters
5 Lost it
6 Sierra __ (Mexican range)
7 Slick stuff
8 Beseeched
9 Gassy talk
10 AK-47 relative
11 *Night Gallery* host
12 Slow sort
13 Irascible
18 __ *Rides Again* (1939 oater)
22 YOU __ HERE
25 Rutgers team color
27 Racetrack boundary
28 Bubbly beverage
29 *Battle Cry* novelist
30 Workshop smoother
32 "Rule, Britannia" composer
35 A pop
37 Cleveland's lake
38 Transmit
40 Golden Pond bird
42 Fish preserver
45 Houston hoopsters
47 Dreamer's opposite
50 Herbal drink
52 Bodega owner
53 *Iliad* king
54 Beatle with the beat
56 James __ Garfield
59 Start of a whaler's cry
61 Fluctuate
62 "Within" word form
63 Senior member
65 Quaint lodging
67 NATO member

ALL IN THE FAMILY

by Rich Norris

ACROSS

1 French cleric
5 Figure skater Thomas
9 Military officials
14 Horse house
15 Impulsive passion
16 Paperboy's itinerary
17 "La Vie en Rose" singer
19 Pianist Watts
20 Trickery
21 Dog star's first name
23 "__ Woman" (Reddy song)
24 Comics teen
28 Experiment locales
30 One way to get the gravy
31 Southwestern native
32 JFK posting
33 Mental acuity
35 Bushy hairdo
39 Potatoes partner
41 Wood-shaping tool
42 Gunslinger's order
43 One of the Three B's
44 Arthur of tennis
45 12/24 is one
46 Fly-by-night sort
48 Curved path
50 Oboist's purchase
51 *Ms.* founder
56 Former Mideast alliance: Abbr.
57 Airline bought by American
58 Turn on an axis

61 Store away
63 Former heavyweight champ
66 Parish donation
67 Getting __ years
68 Horseback game
69 Bad guy's look
70 Does sums
71 Is discontinued

DOWN

1 Under the covers
2 Expressed, as a farewell
3 Yard-sale items
4 Goes in
5 Ocean bottoms
6 Crimson rival
7 Ewe sound
8 Prefix with structure
9 Former German chancellor
10 Director Howard
11 War hero Murphy
12 Proverbial backbreaker
13 Looks (like)
18 Latin adverb
22 Occupied
25 Midwest Indians
26 Nickname
27 Interpret, as tea leaves
28 Mary's follower
29 Carpet coverage
34 The ones here
36 Middle Ages stoneworker
37 Great review

38 Used one's credit
40 Hammer-wielding god
41 Former prime-time drama
47 Become faded
49 Warning signals
50 Do a second draft
51 Quick blasts
52 Livy's language
53 Give a speech
54 Pago Pago locale
55 Word of negation
59 Revealed
60 Son of Seth
62 __ *Stoops to Conquer*
64 Like Perot's party: Abbr.
65 Joke (around)

ACROSS

1 Turkish title
5 DEA agent
9 Fitzgerald forte
13 Yellowish loam
15 Zone
16 Senate gofer
17 Poet's Muse
18 Lab container
19 Scintilla
20 Wilder film subject
23 Chapterplays
24 Meadow foragers
26 Bitterly cold
27 Swizzle stick
29 Miscellaneous collections
32 Curriculum __ (résumé)
34 One __ million
35 Delight
39 Fall mo.
40 Map closeup
41 Golf gadgets
42 Mom and Dad
44 "Harper Valley __"
46 Put the chill on
47 Bomber attribute
51 Skilled golfer
54 Lullaby word
56 Proximate
57 Separate rope strands
58 Conversation filler
59 Foreign-aid org.
60 Cubic meter
61 Tracy's Trueheart
62 Gen. Robert __
63 Carney and Tatum

DOWN

1 Pub staples
2 Garment inserts
3 "__ ho!"
4 Ad hedge
5 Orange feature
6 Diva solos
7 Hindmost
8 Flockhart et al.
9 Keyboard bar
10 Actress Zeta-Jones
11 Past
12 President pro __
14 Super ending
21 "Whoopee!"
22 Fagin, for one
25 Change at Piccadilly
27 Editor's mark
28 Solar products
29 On
30 Battery type
31 Two of the Fondas
32 Astronaut James or Janice
33 Chemical ending
36 Ocean crosser
37 Way in
38 Mythical huntress
43 Engraves with acid
44 Vim
45 Anklebone
47 False alarm
48 Troika complement
49 Part of MTM
50 Core
52 Bluish duck
53 Cultivated grasses
54 Website viewing unit
55 Exploit

ACROSS

1 Entree preceder
6 Cut of marble
10 Yearn for
14 Love, Italian-style
15 Charlie, for one
16 Comics bulldog
17 "Don't bite the hand that __"
19 1984 Peace Prize recipient
20 Kreskin's claim
21 Water trap
22 More permed
24 Dress type
25 Tweety's home
26 Inventor Tull
29 Model T, e.g.
33 WWI danger
34 Seat for 26 Down
35 Clinton alma mater
36 *Rambling Rose* star
37 Carroll cat
38 Arachnid
39 Gumption
40 Bartlett abbr.
41 Mystiques
42 Currier cuts
44 "Play something else!"
45 Cube inventor Rubik
46 Plaster support
47 End a mortgage early
50 Itty-bitty bit
51 Auction action
54 Autobahn vehicle
55 "Strike while the __"
58 For men only
59 __ about

60 Herbert Hoover, for one
61 Resistance units
62 Days of old
63 Timeworn

DOWN

1 It may follow the pitch
2 Biblical prophet
3 Center of Chicago
4 Place of refuge
5 Final course
6 Tour of duty
7 Lie in wait
8 Hill resident
9 Hasselhoff's TV show
10 "A penny saved is __"
11 Needle case
12 Major ender
13 Gloomy
18 Flintstone pet
23 In the past
24 "The pen is mightier __"
25 Schwarzenegger role
26 Judy, for one
27 1975 Pulitzer critic
28 Doughnut-shaped
29 Spanish hands
30 Largest city in Africa
31 Union site
32 *Touched by an Angel* star
34 I-20 may lead to this

37 Song for an Irish tenor
41 Stomach soother
43 CPA's suggestion
44 Grub
46 France's longest river
47 __ doble (Spanish dance)
48 Baseball legend
49 Cheese ball
50 *M*A*S*H* cook
51 Buttons' partner
52 "The wolf __ the door"
53 Turn down
56 Card game
57 Bud's partner

39 GOING TO EXTREMES

by Lee Weaver

ACROSS

1 First Greek letter
6 Likely
9 Onetime Russian ruler
13 Grinding teeth
15 Golfer's goal
16 Military supplies, for short
17 On the whole
19 Fisherman's lure
20 Lack of energy
21 Wraps up
23 Antlered animal
24 Makes a choice
26 Aloof
27 Suppress
28 European cavalryman
31 They're owed
34 Sea duck
36 Singer Rawls
37 Eye part
38 Up and about
39 Grow faint
40 Nog ingredient
41 Quizzes
42 Ade ingredients
43 Member of the AMA
45 Eastern Indians
47 Mata __
48 Ineffectual bombs
49 HS subj.
52 Lasting forever
55 Mail carrier
57 State next to Wash.

58 Arkansas capital
60 Scent finder
61 Kauai keepsake
62 Do a slow burn
63 Editor's notation
64 Gridiron units: Abbr.
65 High-spirited horse

DOWN

1 Easy gait
2 True-blue
3 Thick board
4 Install, as drapes
5 Burdensome
6 IRS mo.
7 Book leaf

8 Mechanical ditchdigger
9 Prohibitions
10 Trick-taking bridge feat
11 Surrounded by
12 Goes bad
14 Inclined ground
18 Free from deceit
22 Tea time, perhaps
25 Made a cut, old-style
27 Milk amts.
29 Topnotch
30 Feels regret
31 Lost power
32 Thus
33 Influential person
35 Cause disorder to

38 How some crops are sprayed
39 Milwaukee's state: Abbr.
41 Ripped
42 Persons holding contracts
44 Archery need
46 Adored ones
49 Bashed, Biblically
50 Hiding place
51 Signed
52 Ages on end
53 Jogging gait
54 Told a whopper
56 Weight allowance
59 "__ the season . . ."

ACROSS

1 Fem.'s opposite
5 Former Tehran rulers
10 Wants to know
14 "It's __ big mistake!"
15 Gem weight
16 "Go away!"
17 Animal parks
18 Computer file-format acronym
19 Simple
20 *Rain Man* actor
23 Kind of committee
24 Pub pint
25 Twelve doz.
28 Actress Winona
32 Prepare a present
34 Shinto, e.g.: Abbr.
37 Hertz competitor
39 Glow brightly
40 *Raintree County* actress
44 Book parts
45 Raise, as a child
46 Santa __, CA
47 Greek goddess of wisdom
49 Took a cut (at)
52 On the other hand
53 That: Sp.
55 "Enough!" to Enzo
59 *The Rainmaker* actor
64 Lacking slack
66 Say
67 Make fun of
68 Stare at
69 To the point
70 Director Kazan
71 Spiders' creations

72 Clear the board
73 Koppel and Kennedy

DOWN

1 Nissan competitor
2 So all can hear
3 Walk through water
4 Pollux's twin
5 Look over quickly
6 Muddle
7 With the bow, in music
8 Israeli seaport
9 Put the kibosh on
10 On the briny
11 *Lost Horizon* land
12 Boxers' stats: Abbr.
13 Sauce source
21 Quite unfriendly
22 Brainy group
26 Talked and talked
27 Puccini performance
29 Small amount
30 At any time
31 Baptism et al.
33 Reason-seeking question
34 Take care of an IOU
35 Make giddy
36 Idea, in the comics
38 Bandleader Artie
41 Scrabble 10-pointer

42 Lou Grant portrayer
43 Nickname for Capote
48 Very perceptive
50 Hoops group: Abbr.
51 Stove nozzle
54 Make changes to
56 Not fresh
57 Mild
58 Sectors
60 Southwestern natives
61 Razor name
62 Robert Stack role
63 Manitoba Indian
64 Stuck vehicle's need
65 Become mature

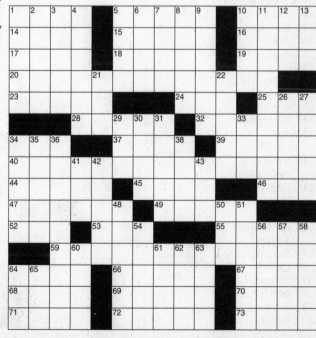

41 "...WITH LOVE"

by Carl Antonelli

ACROSS

1 New England seafood
6 Juxtapose
10 Samms of *Dynasty*
14 Hosiery shade
15 Ascent
16 Placed down
17 Beasts of burden
18 Hebrew month
19 Alternatively
20 Diaghilev offerings
23 __ chi (Chinese discipline)
24 Wilson of *Casablanca*
25 Troy, NY, college
27 Colloquial
30 Plant twice
32 Medicinal
36 Lose influence
37 Dangerous game
42 Singly
43 Devitalized
44 Rocky's wife
47 Martin and Allen
51 Old Olds
52 Soiree snack
56 "__ Believer" (Monkees tune)
57 Vast treeless tracts
61 Mandlikova of tennis
62 Filmmaker Wertmuller
63 Sly peeks
64 Like custard
65 Demonic
66 Shirt size
67 Accountant's income
68 Consider
69 Snaky shapes

DOWN

1 Goes first
2 Certain dress code
3 Where St. Petersburg is
4 Unfolds, poetically
5 Lucy's son
6 "There __ atheists in foxholes"
7 Tolkien hobbit
8 Bar order
9 Worker in a cage
10 Robt. __
11 Abuse
12 Wasted
13 Orange drink
21 Inner sancta
22 Strong soap
26 __ fixe
28 Japanese-American
29 Moo goo __ pan
31 Norse neighbor
33 Hosp. personnel
34 Tax-deferred acct.
35 Joe Friday was one
37 Loud laugh
38 Not yet 18
39 Finagle
40 Overturned
41 Rented
45 Elec. systems
46 Caught
48 Treacherous ones
49 Come out
50 Talks back to
53 Too credulous
54 Musical of "Tomorrow"
55 Sacred song
58 Recites
59 Fashion magazine
60 They're split for soup
61 Magazine magnate, familiarly

42 AWE-FUL

by Patrick Jordan

ACROSS

1 Pacific island republic
5 Open-mouthed
10 Implores
14 Racetrack shape
15 "Chill out!"
16 Way out!
17 Military status
18 Lotto-like game
19 Practice indolence
20 French article
21 Comics superheroine
23 Eyelash thickener
25 Item kicked in a street game
26 __ Girl Friday
27 Fish with a dangerous tail
32 Bob of *Full House*
35 Alack's partner
36 Glamorous Gardner
37 *The Wizard of Oz* character
41 Neuter possessive
42 Annoyance
43 Plow pioneer
44 Book after Ezra
47 Watch chain
48 Actor Kilmer
49 Sunshade
53 Retail district
58 Status follower
59 Made cheddar better
60 The Little Mermaid
61 Knock-knock joke punchlines
62 Canseco of baseball
63 It's said before supper
64 Tortoise vs. hare event
65 Part of NEA
66 German steelworks site
67 Poetic tributes

DOWN

1 Discussion panel
2 Trump ex
3 Curtin and Fonda
4 Variety
5 Shaded recesses
6 Susan's *Thelma & Louise* costar
7 "When I was __ . . ."
8 Glazier's installation
9 Cleansing ritual
10 Hold a membership
11 Student's dread
12 City near the Sphinx
13 British gun
21 Pa Walton portrayer
22 Pallid
24 Culinary luminary
27 Walk through mud
28 Small pastry
29 Glowing review
30 Declare
31 Hillary's alma mater
32 *Wheel of Fortune* option
33 Johnson of *Laugh-In*
34 "Gee whiz!"
35 Braving the waves
38 Overflow
39 Love dearly
40 Singer McEntire
45 Dodges
46 C&W composer Davis
47 Degraded
49 Puzzle part
50 Cheerleading group
51 16 drams
52 Mislays
53 Goya subject
54 Lab assistant of film
55 Silent spot in a score
56 Commits a blooper
57 Farrow et al.
61 Paid player

43 GREAT PERFORMANCES

by A.J. Santora

ACROSS

1 Carbonated drinks
6 Old Turkish title
11 Booster
14 Phone enclosure
15 Playwright Fugard
16 Spanish gold
17 *Your __* (TV oldie)
19 Scale notes
20 Night bird
21 Farm animal
22 Biblical wife
23 Brit. flyers
26 Bike type
28 Artist's surface
29 Mall
31 Nightclub offering
33 Like some temples
35 Italian article
36 Switch positions
37 Run the party
38 One or two
40 *__ rogas* (as you ask: Lat.)
42 Opposite of vert.
44 Not on the network
47 Glitz
50 Aegean area
51 Take the blame
52 Evinced
54 Hood's weapon
55 Impudence
56 However, briefly
57 African snake
59 Palace initials
60 One way to vote
65 Sioux Indian
66 Corner the market
67 McEnroe's ex
68 Wind dir.
69 Coarse files
70 Ungainly

DOWN

1 Network letters
2 Cry of surprise
3 Gambling game
4 Part of Welk's intro
5 Theatrical skill
6 Ballet step
7 Just behind
8 AKC entrant
9 Sewing-machine man
10 Hirt and Gore
11 Previewing
12 "Give him __ for livin'"
13 Reservation neglecters
18 Impresario Ziegfeld
22 Brown of renown
23 LP letters
24 In the style of
25 Runway extravaganza
27 GI rank
28 Treacher's '60s post, familiarly
30 Animal house
32 Norwegian king
34 Take __ the chin
39 "Xanadu" rock group
40 Hope special
41 Obstructs
43 Puts on again
44 Spanish bear
45 Actress Long
46 Snack on
48 Where Cal. and Ore. are
49 Outdo
53 Air Force woman
56 "Take __ Train"
58 Sheet of stamps
60 Armenia, once
61 Goddess of plenty
62 Society-page word
63 Family member
64 Devious

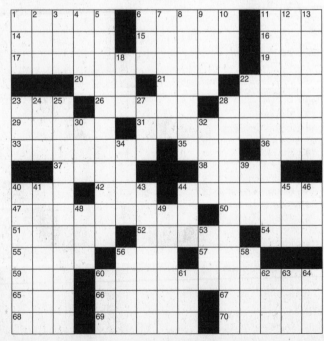

by W.A. Hendricks

ACROSS

1 Vault
5 Portugal neighbor
10 Actress Thompson
14 __ *Well That Ends Well*
15 Witch's revenge
16 Clever remark
17 1978 star-studded movie
20 Ike's area, for short
21 Toast topper
22 Sounded like a lion
23 __ Folly (Alaska)
25 Dinner signal
26 Botanical cell
27 Unrefined metal
28 *The Birth of a Nation* grp.
31 Sneezer's sound
34 __ King Cole
35 Clock numeral
36 1970 Jack Lemmon movie
40 Bridge fee
41 Barn bird
42 "Treat Me Nice" singer
43 Puncturing gadget
44 Business degree: Abbr.
45 Santa __, CA
47 "To __ not to be . . ."
48 Klutzy
52 Looking over
55 Defunct science magazine
56 "Gosh!"
57 1983 Marsha Mason movie

60 Netman Nastase
61 Knight's covering
62 Look surreptitiously
63 "__ Do It" (Porter tune)
64 Requirements
65 Plies a needle

DOWN

1 Ties one's shoe
2 Overjoy
3 Say it's OK
4 Greek letter
5 Berates
6 Most pristine
7 Cartoonist Peter
8 "It __" ("Who's there?" reply)
9 Not as remote from

10 Peer
11 Naturalist John
12 Wee amount
13 Imitated
18 "A Song __" (Carpenters tune)
19 Dover dish
24 "Keep __ head!"
25 Gravy holder
28 Ukraine's capital
29 Soprano Te Kanawa
30 Sign of affection
31 "__ boy!"
32 __ down (eat)
33 War, to Sherman
34 Gridiron letters
35 Relation by marriage

37 Winter transport
38 Man __ (race horse)
39 Vest
44 Restaurant list
45 Rifle adjunct
46 Deed holders
47 Tarries
49 Concur
50 Extend a subscription
51 Students' furniture
52 Actor Jannings
53 New Haven school
54 Sign over a door
55 Treater's words
58 "__ you kidding?"
59 Prosperous times

45 AT THE MARKET

by Bob Lubbers

ACROSS

1 Parcheesi or polo
5 Filet favorite
9 __ in Toyland
14 Double reed
15 Waiter's burden
16 Type of acid
17 Equitable deal
19 City in Tuscany
20 Tee preceder
21 Unctuous
22 Blowfish
23 Impede
25 Noble's partner
27 Golf prop
28 ET fleet
29 Bar bill
32 Big-time
35 Sponsorship
36 Boxer's wear
37 Pie order
39 Use again
41 Hebrides hats
42 Hamburg's river
44 L.A. hoopster
45 Compass pt.
46 Writer James
47 "__ voyage!"
48 French dinner course
50 Accounting plusses
54 Accounting minuses
56 Scout outing
58 Crooner Damone
59 Savory smell
60 Carpool, e.g.
62 Roadside eatery
63 Ended
64 Yemeni port
65 Spine of South America
66 Afternoon parties
67 Crow's home

DOWN

1 Office helper
2 Defame
3 Damp
4 Occupational suffix
5 Pace
6 Exam type
7 Kind of beetle
8 Potato part
9 Petty officers
10 "Get __!"
11 Soup base
12 German article
13 Lasting impression
18 Matador
22 Ordinary writing
24 Iotas
26 Flaming
30 Well qualified
31 Tavern serving
32 Life partner
33 Word of regret
34 Goldfinger's nemesis
35 Did some fishing
36 Meg and Robert
38 *Dancing Class* painter
40 Shuts
43 Activity center
46 Rite places
47 Pastry chefs
49 Evangelist __ Semple McPherson
51 Sidestep
52 Tuckers out
53 __ of a Woman (Pacino film)
54 Baby's word
55 "__ go bragh!"
57 Brainstorm
60 Balderdash
61 Solo of *Star Wars*

46 BOSSY

by Fred Piscop

ACROSS

1 Fedora feature
5 Comic Radner
10 In __ (soon)
14 Casino city
15 At full speed
16 *Time* founder
17 Starter for cumulus
18 Corrupt
19 Mesabi Range deposit
20 Presidential also-ran of '72
23 Whenever one wants
24 Singer Janis
25 Made a federal case
27 Negatively charged
31 Sunday-school lesson
33 *"O Sole __"*
35 Mauna __
36 Antietam general
37 Auto option
44 One in a tight spot?
45 *The Plague* setting
46 Picks out of a lineup
47 Black Sea city
51 Military hierarchy
56 High time
57 Knock for __
58 __ *Three Lives*
59 Pasta, in product names
60 Superman portrayer
61 Tribal tales
62 Ready for business
63 Luckless one
64 __'acte

DOWN

1 Actress Sonia
2 Find a new tenant for
3 Following behind
4 Like Othello
5 Drop-leaf table feature
6 Moslem leader
7 Not of the cloth
8 Surfboard flaw
9 Fats Domino's real first name
10 Property transferrer
11 Duel personality
12 Garbage can, on a PC
13 Gymnast's goal
21 Collagist's need
22 Full of oneself
26 *La __ Vita*
27 Hersey novel locale
28 Void partner
29 Suffix with percent
30 So-so grade
31 Period of duty
32 Card game
33 Roast hosts, for short
34 Lyricist Gershwin
38 Exile of 1979
39 __ Ifni (Moroccan seaport)
40 Tangle up
41 Highway patroller
42 USN bigshot
43 Race distance
48 Art gallery
49 Hagar's dog
50 Venomous viper
51 Hen's pen
52 Fine-tune
53 Grocery stick
54 Opponents
55 Yacht haven
56 Friend, in the 'hood

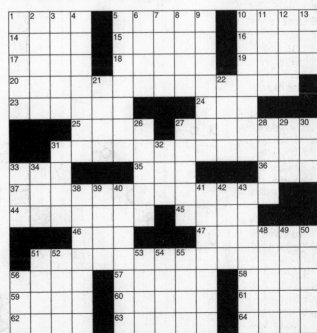

47 YEAR-END READING

by Rich Norris

ACROSS

1 Vending-machine selection
5 Fergie's first name
10 __ Hari
14 Warts and all
15 Central Florida city
16 Overload
17 With 61 Across, Clancy thriller
19 *Star Wars* princess
20 More level-headed
21 With 53 Across, Bellow novel
23 Nacho topping
26 Malt-drying kilns
27 Bargain hunter's destination
31 Light source
32 One of the woodwinds
33 Dashboard gadgets
36 Band item
39 With *The*, Potok book
42 Volcanic output
43 Commercial come-on
44 Dynamic opening
45 Command to a horse
46 Put together
48 Old Greek marketplace
51 Took a chance
53 See 21 Across
55 All thumbs
60 Dole (out)
61 See 17 Across
64 Work without __ (take risks)
65 Combat center
66 Hard to find
67 Hentoff and Turner
68 Sax range
69 Part of a pot

DOWN

1 Musical inspired by Eliot
2 Workplace protection org.
3 Bank claim
4 New York tennis stadium
5 Rob, to Carl
6 Vaudeville unit
7 Floating platforms
8 Hilo hello
9 Mad Hatter guest
10 "American Pie" singer
11 Regions
12 Slangy rejoinder
13 Collect into a pile
18 Bear, to Brutus
22 Throw water on
24 2000 presidential hopeful
25 Like lettuce
27 Senate garment
28 "Down with," in Dijon
29 Ancient invader
30 Use one's peepers
31 Rough
34 Kids' card game
35 Hopeless case
36 Help a hooligan
37 Little more than
38 Give a little poke
40 Water vapor
41 Buddy
45 Receives at the door
47 Polish a story
48 Madison Avenue figure
49 Actress Davis
50 Eight pipers playing
51 Combine company
52 *As You Like It* locale
54 Annoying kid
56 Director Ephron
57 *My Country* author
58 Saucy
59 Family history
62 Yoko __
63 One's wheels

TIMELY REMINDER

by S.N.

ACROSS

1 Desiccate
6 Demographer's goal, perhaps: Abbr.
9 Puts away
14 Miss America gear
15 Age
16 Of tissue
17 One of the Adamses
18 Take the odds
19 LXIII x XVI
20 With 38 and 48 Across, what January 1, 2000 was NOT
23 Handheld computer: Abbr.
24 Chic's partner
25 Teen of the comics
29 Conclusion preceder
31 Letters on a cat-food bag
34 They're cruising together
36 Notable dukedom
37 *Sun-Times* name
38 See 20 Across
39 Lofty abode
40 Produce-scale deduction
41 G&S associate
43 Where a lt.-to-be trains
44 Movie mogul Laemmle
45 Taking it easy
46 The nearest star
47 Part of TGIF
48 See 20 Across
55 Kind of embankment
56 Wildcat strike
57 One lacking hope
59 Like some walls

60 Steamboat Springs gear
61 Free
62 Snack category
63 Animator Avery
64 Indiana's state flower

DOWN

1 School-funding supporter
2 "__ No Sunshine" ('71 tune)
3 Ill-considered
4 Bison hunters of old
5 Unimportant one
6 Tropical butterfly
7 CEO, often
8 NAFTA predecessor
9 Battleground of August 1944
10 Zero role
11 Pastiche
12 Very thin model
13 __ Lanka
21 The same as before
22 Feet, so to speak
25 Vinegary word form
26 African capital
27 Most truckers
28 Engage
29 Antiknock compound
30 Line holder
31 Nero portrayer in *The Story of Mankind*
32 PMs or MPs
33 Shooting game
35 Comment conclusion

36 Fiscal period
39 Misbehaving
41 Artist from Catalonia
42 Wild tale
44 Video-store section
46 Amiable
47 First toon to be on TV
48 St. Petersburg's river
49 Base
50 Wasted
51 Teen's conversation filler
52 Actress Skye
53 Biblical preposition
54 Potsdam pronoun
55 Fleur-de-__
58 *Curious George* author

49 GLACIAL LITTER

by Bob Lubbers

ACROSS

1 Damage
4 Flower part
9 Goliath's challenger
14 Skater Midori
15 Battlefield
16 School: Fr.
17 __ cit. (footnote abbr.)
18 Beach sculptures
20 Singer Paul's family
22 Dry
23 Most close
26 Quickly flashing light
30 Sea nymph
32 Small river
34 Inc., in England
36 Philippine island
38 Sharp fight
39 Corn units
41 Played (with)
43 Flower part
44 Animal scent
46 Dressed as a judge
48 Decade divisions: Abbr.
49 Bank worker
51 Pertaining to leaves
53 Not as fast
55 Farm trucks
58 Sigher's word
60 Afghanistan's capital
61 Small clam
67 Bikini part
68 Evaluated
69 Juan or Eva
70 Allow
71 Newspaper columns
72 RBI and ERA
73 Wide shoe width

DOWN

1 Italian city
2 Make amends
3 Elvis' music
4 Quarterbacks, at times
5 Epoch
6 Top gymnastics rating
7 "No ifs, __ or buts!"
8 Spikes the punch
9 Gobi and Kalahari
10 Play a role
11 Tennessee athlete, for short
12 __ de France
13 __ Moines, IA
19 Part of A&E
21 Exists
24 Chair or bench
25 Malay Archipelago island
27 Mine rocks
28 Barney's wife
29 Pizzeria patron
31 *The __ the Jackal*
33 May honorees
34 For fear that
35 Audio cassettes
37 '40s jazz style
40 Song for one
42 Sandwich shop
45 Bounties
47 *Oliver Twist* author
50 Depend (upon)
52 Alias: Abbr.
54 Coarse files
56 Blender setting
57 Candidate list
59 Editor's mark
61 __-Magnon
62 Prefix for hazard
63 Summer, in France
64 Skelton or Buttons
65 Mouths: Lat.
66 Word of denial

50 SHADES OF MEANING

by Fred Piscop

ACROSS

1 Celery pieces
7 Lhasa __
11 Half a dance's name
14 Difficult to understand
15 MGM founder Marcus
16 Cartoon Chihuahua
17 Major transgression
19 Bond accrual: Abbr.
20 Ceases
21 "__ Excited" (Pointer Sisters tune)
22 In perpetuity
25 *Nature* essayist
27 Be nuts over
28 Dinghy need
30 TV exec Arledge
31 Family member
32 Sing the praises of
34 Educator Horace
35 Angry, with "off"
37 Maine or Montana
39 Cease
42 *Star Trek* captain
44 Kind of dancer
46 Wyo. neighbor
47 Dunne or Papas
49 DC figure
50 Consumer crusader Ralph
52 Edith, to Archie
54 Prophesying woman
56 Rabbit
57 Toon gorilla
59 Gulped down
60 City near Miami

64 Theme of this puzzle
65 Mine finds
66 Negatively charged atoms
67 Lacking moisture
68 Offender, to police
69 Responds to a stimulus

DOWN

1 Anatomical pouch
2 Singing syllable
3 Word form for "height"
4 Roofer's need
5 Motorcycle daredevil
6 Feel in one's bones
7 "__ fair in love . . ."
8 Teen's wall hanging
9 Earth tremor
10 Hold title to
11 Alabama footballers
12 Muppets creator
13 San __ (Texas city, familiarly)
18 Ventilate
21 Actor Jeremy
22 Like a cheetah
23 Garfield's pal
24 Political matriarch
26 Paleozoic, for one
29 "Haste makes waste," e.g.
33 Set, as a price
34 Actress Ryan

36 Grime-covered
38 Throat feature
40 Keats works
41 Links norms
43 Fighter in gray
45 Like some rural bridges
47 Photo-bearing document, often
48 Tear-gas target
49 Gawking sort
51 Oil-rich peninsula
53 Love, to Luigi
55 "Pomp and Circumstance" penner
58 Sound of fright
60 Beat walker
61 Rapper Tone __
62 Medical specialty: Abbr.
63 Conscription org.

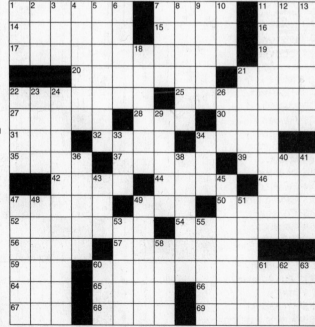

ACROSS
1 Not slack
5 __ and end-all
10 Rotisserie part
14 Scratch target
15 Awesome hotel lobbies
16 The __ 'Clock News
17 Eight furlongs
18 Less forward
19 Lucille Ball film role
20 Daly/Gless cop show
23 Do the pitching
24 Cara of Fame
25 Mechanical man
28 Before the deadline
31 Gershwin et al.
32 Exodus crossing
34 Obliterate, arcade-style
37 '80s TV cop show
40 Moose kin
41 Remains
42 Designer von Furstenberg
43 Asian 21 Down
44 Wine barrels
45 Storage room
48 Praise
50 Lansbury TV series
56 Literary collections
57 San Antonio shrine
58 __ Zapata!
60 Prairie building

61 Florida footballer
62 Primal garden
63 CAT __
64 Do editing
65 Depend

DOWN
1 Dickensian kid
2 Ending for problem
3 West Coast coll.
4 Rex Harrison title role of '47
5 More despicable
6 Gas additive
7 Verdi solo
8 Mortgage, e.g.
9 Frying medium

10 The Bells of __'s
11 Hippie greeting
12 "__, we various passions find . . .": Pope
13 Seeing eye __
21 Tree product
22 Purple color
25 Ready to pick
26 Vocal
27 Spaniel sound
28 '50s auto
29 Clueless phrase
30 Flat rate
32 Take a break
33 First name in whodunits
34 Turns sharply
35 Frenzied
36 Office supplies

38 Eleanor, to Teddy
39 Peruse
43 Makes an offer for
44 Dastard
45 Pile up
46 Greek garment
47 "The flowers that bloom in the spring, __"
48 Sour citrus
49 "And now, __ from our sponsor"
51 Fad
52 Criticize
53 Can't stomach
54 Fisherman's concern
55 Mr. Knievel
59 Whichever

52 GIFTS OF LOVE

by Rich Norris

ACROSS

1 Ruth rival
5 Medal-worthy behavior
10 White-water carrier
14 Oklahoma native
15 Novelist Loos
16 On top of
17 Kegler's target
19 Champagne specification
20 Novel genre
21 Hot
23 Draft drink
24 Expression
26 Annoying ones
28 Intuit
30 Assesses, with "up"
33 __ Paulo
34 Gun owners' grp.
36 Teachers' org.
37 Dermatologist's concern
38 Appalachians, e.g.
42 Dracula feature
43 Line made with a compass
44 Keep greedily
45 Scotch-bottle datum
46 Paragon
48 Medical procedures
52 Old hat
54 Like many spring days
56 __ Haw
57 Belt with twelve signs
60 Volume supporter
62 Ocho __ (Jamaican seaport)
63 Place for a match
65 Diarist Frank
66 Omit in pronunciation
67 Athlete Nastase
68 Foot part
69 Really enjoy
70 Backtalk

DOWN

1 Hooded snakes
2 *My Favorite Year* star
3 Hood and Tell
4 Composer Bartók
5 Carter secretary of state
6 Makes mad
7 Backtalk
8 Singer Redding
9 Talk wildly
10 100 kopecks
11 Relaxing time at Tahoe
12 Soda source
13 Explosive stuff
18 Medical staffer
22 Photo __ (picture sessions)
25 Sportscasting gadget
27 Heir, often
29 Cozy
31 Buddhist discipline
32 Per
35 Somewhat
37 Chef's herb
38 Waiting-room staple
39 Directly confrontational
40 "__ you serious?"
41 Ballpark purchase
42 Short-lived fashion
46 First name in exiles
47 Freudian concept
49 Girl, to an Aussie
50 Sport for 67 Across
51 Rushlike grasses
53 Henry Ford's son
55 Not the gregarious type
58 Burrows and Vigoda
59 Soft drink
61 Actor Kristofferson
62 Cheering sound
64 Sun King's number

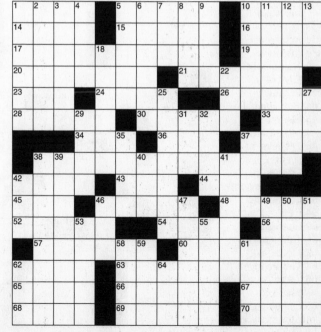

CLEAN HUMOR

by Patrick Jordan

ACROSS

1 Senegal's capital
6 In fine fettle
10 Actress Thompson
14 Select citizenry
15 Do as bidden
16 Soccer score
17 Max and Buddy
18 You'll find it in the reeds
19 Cash for a pot
20 Start of a quip
23 Italian commune
24 "So what __ is new?"
25 Take a chance
28 Flourishes
31 Leg, slangily
34 Lexicographer's study
36 Gym floor protector
37 Barrett of gossip
38 Middle of the quip
42 Some coifs
43 Give in to gravity
44 Subside
45 On the other hand
46 Disbelief of a sort
49 "Yippie!"
50 Gilligan's home
52 True-to-life
54 End of the quip
60 Cutting part
61 Demeanor
62 Nonsensical
64 Gentle rhythm
65 Actress McClurg
66 Himalayan monarchy
67 Pocket janglers
68 Rather and Rostenkowski
69 Speak slowly

DOWN

1 Society newcomer
2 Jai __
3 European capital
4 Up __ (stymied)
5 He might be passive
6 Coolidge's successor
7 French cleric
8 Singer Redbone
9 Canines
10 Old-fashioned oaths
11 Jamaican port
12 Trig or calc
13 Away from the wind
21 Ultimate degree
22 Ernie of golf
25 Berkeley of films
26 Suffix of style
27 In a mocking manner
29 Public persona
30 Winery tank
32 Singer O'Day
33 Sailor's pal
35 Ethane, e.g.
37 Hamlet's catch
39 Held in high regard
40 Ebenezer's expletive
41 Chutney ingredient
46 Tennis term
47 Ryan and Dunne
48 Little Mermaid's home
51 Cancels a dele
53 Cruise ship
54 "Bubbles in the Wine" was his theme
55 Jim Davis dog
56 Opera set in Thebes
57 Corporeal vessel
58 Fertile California valley
59 Chew like a beaver
63 Building extension

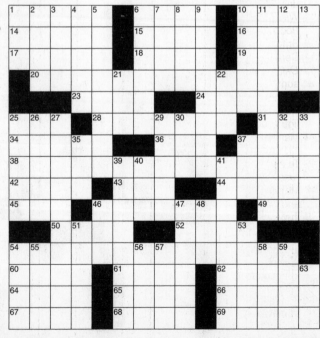

54 GIRL TALK

by Bob Lubbers

ACROSS

1 Dull clang
5 __ avis
9 FDR interior secretary
14 Buck ender
15 Author Bagnold
16 "He's making __, checking it twice"
17 Tinseltown
19 Maxim
20 World's lowest lake
22 Plan part
23 Greek letters
26 Late-night flights
28 Mine: Fr.
29 Overacting actor
32 College military unit: Abbr.
33 Winnie the Pooh creator
35 British noble
37 Cereal grain
40 *Oklahoma!* aunt
41 Sis' sibling
42 Hospital figure
44 Marina del __, CA
45 To no __ (useless)
47 Magnani and Sten
48 Instance
50 Actor Beatty
52 Fender ding
53 Nightly noisemakers
56 Verdi productions
58 Dry riverbed
59 Rocker Pat

62 Combined, as numbers
64 Kids' game
68 Choreographer Agnes de __
69 Poker entry fee
70 Puts to work
71 Take the wrinkles out of
72 Praise
73 Price stickers

DOWN

1 "__, humbug!"
2 Spanish gold
3 Lon __ of Cambodia
4 Prospector's quest
5 Clean again
6 "With a wink and __ . . ."
7 Spanish rivers
8 Viper
9 __ *a Camera*
10 Storage place
11 Diagonally
12 Lauder of cosmetics
13 Comes to a halt
18 Affirmative vote
21 Atmo- cousin
23 More willing
24 What a miss is as good as
25 Pamper
27 Singer Summer
30 Eban of Israel
31 County north of San Francisco

34 Delete
36 Assigned part
38 Yoga posture
39 Exams
43 Offer lower prices
46 Action word
49 Durant and Sharon
51 Like some lines
53 Quagmire
54 Low point
55 Flower part
57 Salary
60 Grandma
61 Aleutian island
63 __ Moines, IA
65 Red __ beet
66 Beer barrel
67 Curved letter

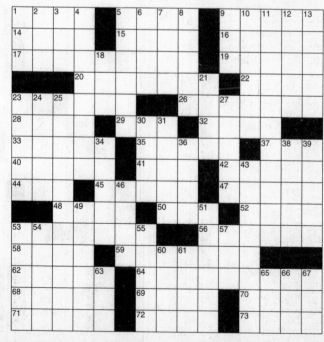

ACROSS

1 Mrs. Tarzan
5 Snug as __ in a rug
9 No longer current
14 Laundry need
15 District
16 Carroll heroine
17 Complaint
18 Dorothy's dog
19 Aggregate
20 By ourselves
23 Sumptuous
24 Pedro's aunt
25 Religious groups
27 "How stupid of me!"
29 Lobbying org.
32 Renoir's hat
33 __ as you are
34 Certain wanderer
35 Tickled pink
38 Southwestern Indians
39 Lubricates
40 Erroll Garner tune
41 Lawn piece
42 Imitate
43 Cabbie's income
44 Continent south of Eur.
46 Let __ (reveal)
47 Green-card holder
53 Imp
54 Appearance
55 Test
57 Shaquille of basketball
58 "Encore!"
59 Quote
60 One of the Osmonds
61 "The __ the limit!"
62 Harrow rival

DOWN

1 Triangular sail
2 Vicinity
3 Playwright Coward
4 Strong-arm guys
5 Montezuma's people
6 Telephone kiosk
7 "Do __ others . . ."
8 School subject: Abbr.
9 Singer LaBelle
10 Hi, in HI
11 Location
12 The Lion King villain
13 Moray
21 Eliot Ness foe
22 Maria Shriver's aunt
25 Take care of
26 Goofed
27 Arthur Conan __
28 Diamond arbiters
29 Sheriff's men
30 Lends a hand
31 Buffalo Bill
32 Air conditioner numbers: Abbr.
33 Cut out coupons
34 Toupee
36 Get on
37 PC-to-PC communication
43 Some cereals
44 Thai, for one
45 Young mare
46 Tale
47 Nevada city
48 All tied up
49 Shade trees
50 Niche
51 Way out
52 Kosovo force
53 Cabinet dept.
56 Chess pieces

FOR CRYING OUT LOUD

by Fred Piscop

ACROSS

1 Actress Sonia
6 Sprout up
10 Church service
14 Suez Canal traveler
15 Ready to eat
16 Composer Satie
17 "__ All Ye Faithful"
18 Pub offerings
19 Chenin Blanc, e.g.
20 Crybaby's cold symptom?
22 Tatter's product
23 Choice word
24 Beginning
26 Enjoy the library, perhaps
30 Grant portrayer
32 Plaster backing
33 Dixie bread
35 1945 summit site
39 __ spumante
40 Like cheap speakers
42 Debtors' debts
43 Did superbly
45 Naldi of silents
46 Women in habits
47 Conjure up
49 Make tracks
51 Ibsen character
54 Came down with
55 Caron role
56 Crybaby's recreational area?
63 Fruity drinks
64 Botch up

65 Slackened
66 Isn't able to
67 Concerning, in legalese
68 "Slammin' Sammy"
69 Tackles' neighbors
70 Within earshot
71 Grid great Bradshaw

DOWN

1 Italy's shape
2 Highly caloric
3 Sunburn soother
4 Prized items
5 Pugs' venues
6 Turkey topper
7 Churn up
8 Autobahn auto
9 Smith's partner
10 Crybaby's supply carriers?
11 Coloraturas' tunes
12 As of
13 Target sport
21 All thumbs
25 Road reversal
26 Gil __ (Le Sage novel)
27 Hasty
28 Snorkel's pooch
29 Crybaby's beverage selections?
30 Musical based on a strip
31 Shipped
34 Sty cry

36 Vulgarian
37 Ignore, with "out"
38 Org.
41 Vulgarian
44 Night before
48 Starting place
50 Not moving
51 Sugar-coated
52 Actor Quinn
53 Liquor category
54 Errand runner
57 "__ of your beeswax!"
58 Mrs. Copperfield
59 Glazier's unit
60 Mouse manipulator
61 TV producer Norman
62 Countercurrent

POP COUNTDOWN

by Patrick Jordan

ACROSS

1 Coast Guard woman
5 British buggy
9 Up to this point
14 In vigorous health
15 Mislay
16 Ready to spit nails
17 Copiously
18 "__ boy!"
19 Biblical spy
20 "Closer to God" group
23 The Jets, to the Sharks
24 "And others," briefly
25 What a flatterer appeals to
28 Southern senator
30 More like Croesus
32 Fish-cake fish
35 "Rag Doll" group
38 *Lucky Jim* author
40 Stimpy's buddy
41 Novillero's opponent
42 "Dancing Machine" group
47 Cub-scout unit
48 Freed, in a way
49 Pike's discovery
51 Pop star Peeples
52 Beatles' meter maid
55 Says "Howdy!" to
59 "Joy to the World" group
62 Savory scent
64 "__ lay me down . . ."

65 Kite catcher in *Peanuts*
66 Candidate in '92 and '96
67 Qualified
68 Close by
69 Cannes cup
70 Sergeant's supper
71 Ladder rung

DOWN

1 Writer Alexander
2 Monty Python member
3 *Sing __ With Mitch*
4 Go over again
5 Makes a date of it
6 Univ. marchers
7 __ *World Turns*
8 Intended
9 Palermo's island, to the locals
10 Paperless exam
11 Untruth
12 Snacked on
13 Yank's foe
21 Brotherhood org.
22 Interlaken's river
26 Literary class
27 Ex of Rita
29 Chance to play
31 Winter hrs. in Waukegan
32 Louisiana cuisine
33 Muscat resident
34 Autocrats
36 TKO caller
37 Scissors sound

39 Compete in a slalom
43 Cut sharp notches into
44 *Garfield* dog
45 Side dishes
46 Win through hard work
50 Rock's Richards and Moon
53 Midmorning hour
54 Sun-dried brick
56 Long-plumed wader
57 Opposite of 68 Across
58 Expensive
60 Group ins. cos.
61 Hooting hunters
62 Quick to learn
63 Stephen of *The Crying Game*

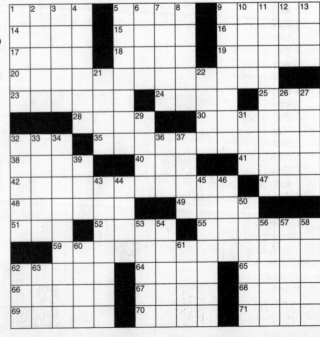

58 LONG SHOTS

by Thomas W. Schier

ACROSS
1 Graphic beginning
5 Tie down
11 Align
13 Typewriter part
14 Irish Free State, in Ireland
17 Cup edge
18 Volcanic one
19 Card game
20 "See __, pick it up . . ."
22 Puts on the nosebag
23 What bonds signify
24 Spite
26 No's colleagues: Abbr.
27 Artificial lightning creator
28 Kid being watched, perhaps
30 Bagpipe kin
32 Bug group
34 Alarm clock setting, maybe
35 Skilled speaker
38 *Animal House* college
39 Acquire
41 Indecorous exhibition
42 *Corro*, in Colombia
43 Lens setting
45 Tie holders

46 Cinematographers' org.
47 "The more __, the less he spoke . . .": *Punch*
49 "That's amazing!"
50 Ultimatum
53 Cover over
54 They're often recalled
55 Hardens
56 Following

DOWN
1 Something insignificant
2 Smallest cont.
3 Coordinate
4 Lacking
5 Gets the lead out
6 Disney's middle name
7 Wag
8 All-purpose truck
9 She has lots to show you
10 Elevate
11 Asian capital
12 Ending for addle
14 Croats, e.g.
15 It's used in oral exams
16 Half of NB
21 Odd
23 Take away
25 Poet's concern
27 Duffers, once per hole
29 Poetic adverb

31 Pou __ (vantage point)
33 Garment makers, jocularly
34 Cold winds
36 __ *Not Enough*
37 Adjust
38 Arbitrary order
40 ". . . and __ a goodnight"
43 Of an unborn
44 Dress smartly
47 Rent
48 Lord's lady
51 She had a little lamb
52 __ populi

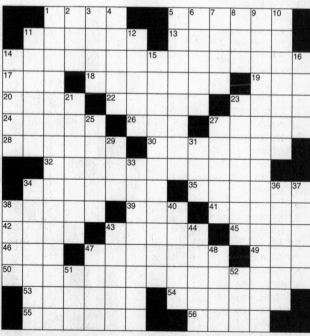

by Lee Weaver

ACROSS
1 Spaghetti, e.g.
6 That woman
9 Large bodies of water
13 Needed liniment
14 Ireland, in poetry
16 Otherwise
17 Coffee add-in
18 *The King* __
19 Water barrier
20 Part of AT&T: Abbr.
21 Headed for trouble
24 Angler's devices
26 Yearned
27 Autumn apple
29 Secluded valleys
31 Lotion ingredient
32 Take steps
34 Cry audibly
37 Accustom
39 Entered the race
40 Performers' platform
42 __ "King" Cole
43 Uncertainties
46 Leg joint
47 Has an elegant supper
48 Destroys slowly
50 Use the rink
52 Comprehend
53 Municipal meetings ordinance
56 Sigh of contentment
59 Asian nursemaid
60 Artist Salvador
61 Containing nothing

63 Glowing review
64 Straight __ arrow
65 Velocity
66 High cards
67 Model Carol
68 Little Pigs count

DOWN
1 Formal agreement
2 Land unit
3 Pays
4 Coffee alternative
5 Think highly of
6 Coin-flip call
7 Fish-eating flier
8 Roller coaster, e.g.

9 Family cars
10 Upper crust
11 Made inquiries
12 Soothsayer
15 __ in the bud (prevented)
22 Tennis court dividers
23 Claret and port
25 Computer owner
27 April forecast
28 Forearm bone
29 Takes rudely
30 Fiber fluff
33 Undeniable
34 Wood smoother
35 Curved molding
36 Drones and queens

38 Archie's spouse
41 Boxing wins
44 New York lake
45 Blood components
47 Punctuation marks
49 Least refined
50 Poison shrub
51 Tart thief
52 Sparkle
53 Poet Teasdale
54 Space shuttle grp.
55 Airline to Israel
57 Suit to __
58 __ Park (FDR's home)
62 Speedometer letters

MEN AND BEASTS

by Bob Lubbers

ACROSS

1 Big party
5 Singer Midler
10 Fizzling-out sound
14 Double-reed instrument
15 Galactic visitor
16 Cash in Cassino, once
17 Legendary Alabama coach
19 Gen. Robert __
20 Uses a sieve
21 Imagined
23 __ Cruces, NM
24 Equals
25 Gives temporarily
28 Sailor
29 Cartoonist Goldberg, et al.
33 "__ Gotta Crow"
34 __ Lingus
35 Extremely
36 Harlem Globetrotters star
40 Complete
41 Dennis or Doris
42 GI address
43 Got to one's feet
44 *Little Women* sister
45 Struck a stance
47 Philbin of TV
49 High mountain
50 Wool gatherer
53 Populates
57 Group of horses
58 PGA star
60 __ Major
61 Native New Zealander
62 Narrow cut
63 Young men
64 Overact
65 Has a bite

DOWN

1 Ducks for apples
2 Back up a holdup
3 Fly high
4 Harbinger
5 Farm structures
6 Actor Ron, et al.
7 Spanish aunt
8 Delicate
9 __ nous (between us)
10 Enjoyment
11 Movie
12 On the house
13 __ up (prepared to drive)
18 Diagonal
22 Actor Flynn
24 Thankgiving Day events
25 Citrus fruits
26 Happening
27 "Fab!"
28 __ Aviv
30 Altar enclosures
31 Avoid a big wedding
32 Church council
34 Amazement
35 The heavens
37 Museum animal displays
38 *Law &* __
39 Joplin composition
44 Aaron's sister
45 Clear away snow
46 Go against
48 "__ to the Church on Time"
49 Eagle's nest
50 Bump a toe
51 Role model
52 As __ as ABC
53 Spunky
54 Falana or Albright
55 Check copy
56 Retired Air France planes
59 Muck

61 SHTICK FIGURES

by Patrick Jordan

ACROSS

1 Heavy knock
6 Golf-course measure
10 Spew forth
14 Math comparison
15 "Oh!"
16 Inventor Sikorsky
17 He inspired *Cats*
18 31 Across trademark
20 Snakelike swimmer
21 Cleopatra's killer
23 NBC emcee
24 More formal
27 Actress Dahl
31 Slapstick group, with "The"
33 Minstrel's song
35 Passport stamp
36 Acquire
37 Cavalry sword
39 Strain
40 Vacuum tube type
42 __-Locka, FL
43 Guided weapon, for short
45 Unspecified amount
46 31 Across trademark
51 Garden shrub
52 Rescuers
56 __ cost (free)
58 Comic Louis
59 Gross, less expenses
60 31 Across trademark
64 Chest wood
66 Carries laboriously
67 Nobelist Wiesel
68 Give the slip to
69 Oceanic ice
70 Twosome
71 Catch a catnap

DOWN

1 Cornered
2 In better health
3 Serviceable
4 "O Sole __"
5 Saltpeter ingredient
6 "Hooray!"
7 "__ was saying . . ."
8 Film holder
9 Vanquishes
10 *American __* (Gere movie)
11 Sound of discomfort
12 Foster Brooks persona
13 Day divs.
19 Tactical advancement
22 Knight's title
25 Eyelid problem
26 Overhauls
28 Incite to action
29 In dire straits
30 Italian noble surname
32 Pack complement
33 Bolivia's capital
34 Philippine fiber
37 Living-room piece
38 __ the occasion
39 TV sked abbr.
41 *Othello* villain
44 Moved like a robot
47 Pass, as time
48 Caused torment to
49 Harvard wall climber
50 Auntie's daughters
53 Excessive
54 *The Cloister and the Hearth* author
55 Throat bug, briefly
57 Word on some shampoo bottles
60 Santa helper
61 *The King and I* name
62 One of a Freudian trio
63 Actress Long
65 Annex

THE INSIDE DOPE

by Fred Piscop

ACROSS

1 Donnybrook
7 Warty one
11 Hans of Dadaism
14 Smitten
15 Cartoon pooch
16 Neckline shape
17 18th-century theater fare
19 Unlock, poetically
20 Sprinter's assignment
21 Kitchen gadget
23 Did major editing
27 Rogues
29 Seinfeld pal
30 Emulated
31 Actress Raines
32 Mud __ (kind of wasp)
34 Roulette bet
37 Move like a crab
39 Beehive State athlete
40 Custodian, for short
42 "__ Beso" (Anka tune)
43 Tender touch
46 Slots spot
47 From __ to post
49 Staccato's opposite
51 Homo sapiens, e.g.
53 Hung in the air
54 Appear suddenly
55 Toddler's glassful
56 Bernese mount
57 Prepared, as mussels
64 __ Dawn Chong
65 Viscount's superior
66 Greek moon goddess
67 Create a snafu
68 "__ me in!"
69 All the rage

DOWN

1 Bit of baloney
2 Genetic letters
3 The works
4 Army rank: Abbr.
5 Land of Arthurian legend
6 Under
7 Drink too much
8 Praiseful poem
9 Go public with
10 Non-PC letter opener
11 Guacamole base
12 Ward off
13 Jury members
18 Change machine insert
22 Zamboni's milieu
23 One of the Boys of Summer
24 Designer Perry
25 Redford role of '75
26 Yemeni money
27 Rite wear
28 Do a takeoff on
30 More cunning
33 Pervasive atmospheres
35 Al __ (pasta order)
36 Dickens character
38 Surpassed
41 The munchies, e.g.
44 Rathskeller quaff
45 Most obtuse
48 Post-OR place
50 Artful dodger
51 Bowler's mark
52 Diametrically opposed
53 Easter entrée
55 NYSE's street
58 __ kwon do
59 Epoch
60 Bullring "bravo!"
61 Confident solver's tool
62 It may be living
63 Roll-call dissent

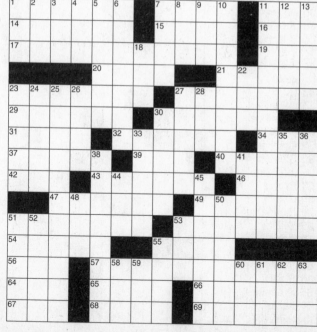

63 OVER YOUR HEAD

by A.J. Santora

ACROSS
1 Band aids
5 Apr. figurers
9 Running, as water
14 Filet fish
15 Emporium event
16 Marriage vows
17 Invigorating
19 Snappish
20 Cole Porter musical
22 Make sure of
23 Wind dir.
24 Pear plant?
28 Polite answer
30 Weight rebate
32 Clark of country
33 __ the bud
35 Relaxed
38 Jet Pilot flew in this
41 Diary
42 Roper's need
43 Uris character
44 As above
46 British flashlight
50 Student teacher
53 Crowd
55 Coach Parseghian
56 '90s fad
59 Addis __
62 Old Oldses
63 Surrendered
64 Suit to __
65 Dreadful
66 Jazz pianist Wilson
67 Tykes
68 For the asking

DOWN
1 Neat __
2 Where Prince Albert rules
3 Aircraft
4 Ward of *Once and Again*
5 DC-based TV channel
6 Sad
7 Inter __
8 Division
9 Cobwebby place
10 FBI director under Clinton
11 Spanish article
12 Giant great
13 Kid's mantra
18 Retired professors
21 Stair parts
25 Part of UAR
26 Optimistic
27 Indigo, e.g.
29 __ time flat
31 Bracelet place
34 Kal-Kan competitor
36 Treaty subject
37 Switch ender
38 "Ol' Man River" composer
39 Give forth
40 Whined
41 Merry month in Paris
45 Type of insurance
47 NFL player
48 Cooking style
49 Bother
51 Receded
52 Set to go
54 Orchestra members
57 Greek letter
58 Bad golf shot
59 Do something
60 Themed gathering
61 Increase, with "to"

64 UP, UP AND AWAY

by Lee Weaver

ACROSS

1 24-hour cash source: Abbr.
4 Ottoman Empire governor
7 Running fast
13 Bishop's domain
15 Aviatrix Earhart
16 Type of number
17 Star system
18 Devoted to
21 Latin existence
22 Santa __, CA
23 Frolic
27 Seasonal laziness
31 Tea holder
34 Lacking slack
35 Let up, as a storm
36 Food
38 Calms
40 "__ is an island . . ."
41 Withered
42 Asner and Bradley
43 Join the fun
46 Poems of praise
47 Water, in Montreal
48 Headliner
52 Trusting act
56 Chewed on a bone
60 June 14th
61 Auto appendage
62 Pistol or rifle
63 Do a slow burn
64 French holy woman: Abbr.
65 Untruth

DOWN

1 Pueblo material
2 Novices: Var.
3 __ operandi
4 Relax, as rules
5 Biblical brother
6 Puppy's cry
7 Disheveled
8 Asian nursemaid
9 Animation frame
10 Dockworker's org.
11 Decide against
12 In a merry mood
14 Film, in France
19 Bide one's time
20 Small hotel
23 McEntire of country
24 Egg-shaped
25 Rationed (out)
26 The media
27 Dictation pro
28 Tin __ Alley
29 Wagon-wheel path
30 Lost color
31 Bluegrass instrument
32 Vocally
33 "__ a break!"
37 Atlas pages
38 Ocean
39 Be inaccurate
41 Chicken noodle, e.g.
44 Sewing-kit item
45 Ram's remark
48 Turkey-stuffing herb
49 Kind of wave
50 Video-game name
51 Versify
52 Wife of Jacob
53 Switch positions
54 Dart
55 Paying passenger
56 Auto fuel
57 Born: Fr.
58 "__ you sure?"
59 Punster, for one

by Rich Norris

ACROSS

1 The two of them
5 Employed
9 Nonsense
14 Minuscule amount
15 Basketballer Archibald
16 Swiss cheese features
17 Prosecutes to the hilt
20 Big name in chocolate
21 Share (in)
22 Before, poetically
23 Barbecue site
25 Med. employees
26 Hill climber
27 Recedes
29 Football stand
32 Dolt
35 Chimney passage
36 Month named for Caesar
37 Detailed information
40 Gets ready to fire
41 __ of Our Lives
42 Annoyed
43 57 Down catchers
44 Quote from
45 Show curiosity
46 Derek and Jackson
47 Facts and figures
49 Tiny, in Troon
52 Consider for a while
56 Lower in esteem
58 Makes a recommendation

60 Be in concurrence
61 Salon order
62 Steinbeck migrant
63 Track contests
64 Sound unit
65 Gives permission to

DOWN

1 Cleanse
2 None of the above
3 Yankee manager
4 Managed care grps.
5 Remove from office
6 Woodland deity
7 Biblical verb ending

8 Full of meaning
9 Rose stickers
10 Alex Haley novel
11 Actress Chase
12 Mountain top
13 Italy's Villa d'__
18 Rhetorical question
19 Like some wire
24 Not on time
26 Current units
28 Hot-dog holders
29 Ankara resident
30 "So what __ is new?"
31 Watched warily
32 Con game
33 Bit of wood
34 Deli meats
35 Campus club

36 Loser
38 "The Wizard of Menlo Park"
39 Approved for travel, in a way
44 Clones, e.g.
45 In
46 Attack on all sides
48 Squirrel stash
49 Wheel part
50 Be worthy of
51 Where the Amazon begins
52 Unwanted E-mail
53 Racing sled
54 French 101 verb
55 Short snoozes
57 Missing GI
59 Word form for "earth"

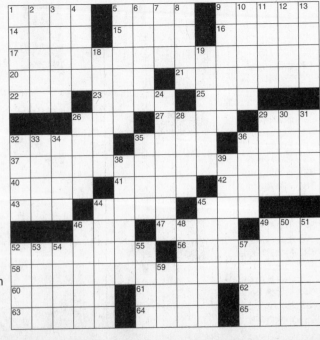

66 IN DEW TIME

by Bob Lubbers

ACROSS

1 Sustenance
5 Take rudely
9 Settee
13 Road divisions
15 __ majesty (high crime)
16 Ruthless ruler
17 Where __ (trendy place)
18 Grub
19 Yours and mine
20 Flynn film of '38
23 Actress Stella
24 Aches and pains
26 Profit
27 Temperature scale
30 The chills
33 Swipe
35 Churchill gesture
36 Frankie Carle's theme
40 Rapscallion
41 Actress Phoebe
42 Rara avis
43 Soup servers
45 Part of USNA
47 Land of the Incas
48 Vie
52 Maxfield Parrish work
56 Autumn pear
58 Moro of Italy
59 Radical Hoffman
60 Drive the getaway car
61 Napoli notes, once
62 Tennis star Monica
63 Jar tops
64 More or __
65 Scarlet and ruby

DOWN

1 Dart about
2 Pledges
3 Beginning
4 Numbing agent
5 Senator in space
6 Gathers in
7 The Charles' terrier
8 First-rate
9 Saloon seats
10 Weissmuller costar
11 Way off
12 __ *gratia artis*
14 Barrel piece
21 Moist
22 Lunar valley
25 "Blue __ Shoes"
27 Average grades
28 Knack for music
29 Soothsayer
30 __ were
31 Spoil
32 Wrinkled
33 Match parts
34 Mao __-tung
37 Get slippery
38 __ Andreas fault
39 When most Scorpios were born
44 Builds
45 Compass dir.
46 Razor brands
48 Nautical offs.
49 Symphonic reeds
50 Aristocratic
51 Dehydrated
53 Lofty
54 Writer Wiesel
55 Famous loch
56 Dance, in France
57 Japanese sash

RISKY BUSINESS

by Patrick Jordan

ACROSS

1 Mint or mustard
5 Stockroom platform
9 Some earrings
14 Spread in sticks
15 Sported
16 Prevention unit
17 Engrossed
18 Pennsylvania county
19 Any Buddy Holly record
20 Trite comeback
23 Hebrew school
24 Gets more weaponry
27 Saint-Tropez *saison*
28 Hoo-ha
30 Eavesdrop electronically
31 Stow cargo
33 Swing around
34 *Reginald* author
35 Linus' constant companion
38 WWW address starter
39 Crooner Jerry
40 West and Busch
41 In the past
42 Lean and powerful
43 Ribboned tree of song
44 Madison follower
46 Inattentiveness
50 Spy film catchphrase
53 "Father of Psychoanalysis"
55 Catch a glimpse of
56 Victor's outburst
57 Nautical "Nonsense!"
58 Scheherazade offering
59 "Toodle-oo!"
60 Do-nothing
61 Earned a ticket
62 Orbs

DOWN

1 Like the polo-playing set
2 Send into ecstasy
3 Bank take-backs
4 Made a mess of
5 Turn suddenly
6 Divided country
7 Spring bloom
8 Profound
9 10 Down resident
10 Oral Roberts U. site
11 Attempt
12 One-fifth of MMMV
13 "Get it?"
21 He writes bad checks
22 Bay window
25 Fabricates
26 Roasting skewer
28 With cunning
29 Cookie-dough container
31 Release
32 Anne Brontë pseudonym
33 Old Glory symbol
34 First-aid emergency
35 Counterfeit
36 Like Yale's walls
37 Accumulate
42 "Superstition" singer
43 Took orders from
45 Cheek reddener
46 More than adequate
47 "Forget it!"
48 Franklin's bill
49 Authors Ferber and Buchanan
51 Namath's first pro team
52 PDQ
53 Justice Dept. agcy.
54 Disencumber

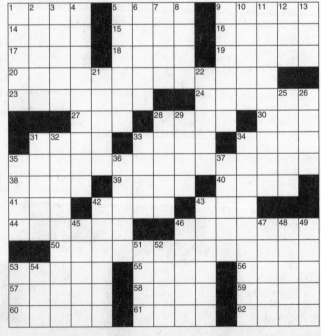

68 SPEAKING LITERALLY

by David A. Rosen

ACROSS

1 Laugh-track snippets
6 Joule-coulomb
10 Missile home
14 Ten-percenter
15 *In perpetuum*
16 Fall preceder
17 Poet __ Jones
18 Comic Rudner
19 Ex of Burt
20 Nationwide
23 Byzantine figure
24 Tons
25 Relinquish
28 Brooklet
30 "__ unto him!" (formulaic curse)
34 USPS bldg.
35 Ceremonial staff
36 Spa patron, often
37 Love song of 1934
40 Snowy straightaway
41 Lord of Ferrara
42 Biting breeze
43 LP player
44 Roguish
45 "The wolf __ the door"
46 Start of some juice names
48 A billion years
50 Sarge's "Hurry up, lazybones!"
57 Breathing space
58 *Inter* __
59 Dye used in cosmetics
60 Exchange premium

61 Bagpiper's wear
62 Organic compound
63 Bird on a Canadian $1 coin
64 Naturalness
65 In the future

DOWN

1 Moiety
2 "Ain't She Sweet?" writer
3 Man of the hour
4 Lack of norms
5 Rover's retrieval
6 Archie Comics character
7 Aries, to Caesar
8 __ *Weapon*
9 Shadow
10 Seceded
11 Inflexible
12 *Metropolis* director
13 Ear-related
21 Liturgical scrolls
22 Not at all
25 Firm and fresh
26 Geological episode
27 "Tiny Bubbles" crooner
29 Archimedean machine
31 Some collars
32 Minister under Stalin
33 Emulate Kilauea
35 City of India
36 Hearkened, old-style
38 Midday event
39 Up the ante
44 Medieval name for England
45 "When __, do as . . ."
47 Come to
49 West Indies sorcery
50 Autumnal birthstone
51 NASA decision
52 The Andrews Sisters, e.g.
53 Portrait medium
54 "The doctor __"
55 Pres. title
56 Mini revelation

69 MATERIALISM

by Lee Weaver

ACROSS

1 Furnish food for a party
6 Heavy weights
10 "In what way?"
13 Overhead
14 Spoken exams
16 Wrath
17 Home storage area
19 Afternoon social
20 Made a deceptive move
21 Aquarium device
23 Musician's gift
24 Part of MIT: Abbr.
25 Lingers
29 Some mollusks
32 Self
33 Witch hunt town
35 __ B. Anthony
36 Life stories, for short
38 Existed
40 Evergreen tree
41 Koran creator
43 __ La Mancha
45 Meadow
46 Mark again
48 Smiled smugly
50 Water, in Madrid
51 Travel-planning grp.
52 Has in mind
55 More gusty
59 Sound of awe
60 Circus confection
62 Western Indian
63 Lift with effort
64 Bert's buddy
65 Sunday address: Abbr.
66 Madrid matrons: Abbr.
67 Mountain curves

DOWN

1 Leg part
2 Irish Rose lover
3 Author Morrison
4 Tied (up)
5 Summer cottages
6 Tattled (on)
7 Spanish gold
8 Space shuttle grp.
9 With ice pellets falling
10 Use a parachute
11 Sandwich cookie
12 Wash-and-__
15 Tension
18 Breakfast bowlful
22 Misbehave
25 Exclude
26 Flexible
27 Indulge in daydreaming
28 *Ghostbusters* goo
29 Seer's signs
30 Indian queen
31 Golf great Sam
34 Perón of Argentina
37 *Beetle Bailey* character
39 Field of influence
42 Part of the hip
44 Engaged woman
47 Pedestal parts
49 Air-traffic detectors
52 Debtor's markers
53 Scale symbol
54 Constellation part
55 Troubles
56 Motels
57 Singer Adams
58 Deli loaves
61 New Deal agency: Abbr.

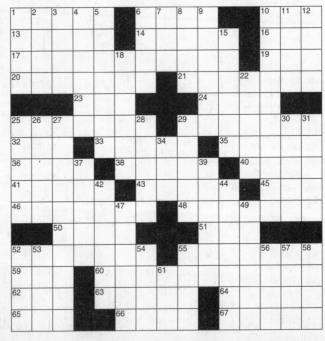

YOUR HIT PARADE

by Bob Lubbers

ACROSS

1 Surmounting
5 Big mess
10 Spring bulb
14 Henry VIII's sixth
15 Book leaves
16 Meditate
17 Mishmash
18 Trapper's unit
20 Dundee native
22 Assistants
23 Unused
24 Wheat piece
27 Eritrea's capital
30 Chess sequence
34 Massage
35 Scurrilous
37 Stink ending
38 Juice drink
39 Portuguese wine
41 *Annie Get Your __*
42 Pepper grinder
44 Soup serving bowl
45 "Absolutely!"
46 Washington's river
48 End-of-term exams
50 Hindu social division
52 Have being
53 Brown ermine
56 Italian cheese
61 Medicine chest tube
64 Vincent Lopez theme
65 Wood trimmer
66 Revere
67 Vaudeville spots
68 "Who __ there?"
69 Desert wanderer
70 Three-person card game

DOWN

1 Mil. addresses
2 Baby powder
3 Certain band of stars
4 For now, for short
5 Canned meat name
6 Zola work
7 Maturing
8 Not masc.
9 2002 Winter Olympics host
10 Encroach
11 Regretted
12 Capri or Wight
13 Gels
19 Put down
21 Bee bunch
25 Comfort
26 Diplomat Gromyko
27 Sound man's concern
28 Lassos
29 Carry off illegally
31 Diamond-patterned footwear
32 Pouting grimaces
33 Eternities
34 Sloping walkway
36 __ Lingus
40 Vietnam part
43 Finds
47 High-school subject
49 Sports palaces
51 __ salts
53 Male deer
54 Fuss
55 Seep
57 Shaver brand
58 Marsh plant
59 BC neighbor
60 Cartoonist Thomas
62 Criticize
63 *Much __ About Nothing*

GUY TALK

by Thomas Fuller

ACROSS

1 Ballroom favorite
6 Night-table light
10 Show-biz failure
14 Not from Earth
15 Word form for "right"
16 Buckeye State
17 Tourist magnet
18 Spirit of the sea
20 "__ silly question . . ."
21 Asian holiday
22 Neil and Carly
23 John of rock
25 Cancel publication of
26 Word origin
28 Symbol of America
32 Doughboys' milieu: Abbr.
33 Bear-book writer
35 Mezzo Frederica Von __
36 Swizzle
38 Fall quaff
40 Blinds part
41 Seaborne flock
43 Eyelashes
45 Sweater size: Abbr.
46 February flyer
48 Mini-Me player Verne
50 Step __ (rush)
51 Transfer image
52 Ariel of Israel
55 From Vienna: Abbr.
56 Runs well
59 Nose nipper
61 Amass, in a way
62 Calamitous
63 Adequate
64 Medieval guild
65 Winter vehicle
66 Dancer's clickers
67 Inception

DOWN

1 Doll's word
2 Pub servings
3 Potent potable
4 Soothe
5 __ shoestring
6 Shade of green
7 "I smell __!"
8 VH1 rival
9 Cathartic
10 Spurts of activity
11 "Horrors!"
12 Appearance
13 One reported to
19 *Four __ in a Jeep* (1944 film)
21 Pick-me-up
24 Male turkey
25 Prepare to propose
26 Moderated
27 Aquarium dweller
28 Took back, in a way
29 Teacakes
30 Proverb
31 Just over a yard
34 On the law's side
37 Saved some wine for later
39 Ceremonial goings-on
42 "Made glorious summer by this __ York"
44 Circle part
47 Cedar affliction
49 Hawaiian islander
51 "__ faithful child"
52 Highest legal degs.
53 Cab signal
54 Heartland unit
55 Letters of urgency
57 Erato, for one
58 Imbroglio
60 Russian river
61 Greek letter

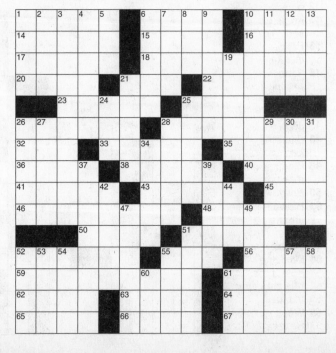

72 VERBAL CAUTIONS

by Rich Norris

ACROSS

1 Common sense
7 Laugh-a-minute type
14 Bobbing on the waves
15 Mother-of-pearl source
16 "Be careful what you say!"
18 Well-built
19 Throat trouble
21 See 57 Across
24 Elongated swimmer
25 Volcanic output
27 *Mer* contents
28 Pitcher Hershiser
30 Seaman
32 Etta of comics
33 More like the Marx Brothers
36 Period of indulgence
38 "Don't tell anyone!"
42 Actress Veronica
43 Jewish law
45 Simon Legree type
48 Exec's request
50 Brown rival
51 Have regrets about
52 Farm crawler
53 Happy moments
56 Crafty
57 With 21 Across, Nile structure
59 Imbibe
61 "Keep quiet!"
67 Senator Dirksen

68 Sings like Crosby
69 Moral sense
70 Type of sugar

DOWN

1 Carpenter's tool
2 Writer's deg.
3 PC key
4 Mythical birds
5 Sierra Nevada lake
6 *Je ne sais quoi*
7 Showy ornament
8 Shortened, as a dict.
9 Group of whales
10 Walk through water
11 Racetrack figure

12 Main course
13 Use the microwave
17 Monet medium
20 Place in position
21 Baker's amt.
22 Mideast resident
23 Computer list
25 Laddie Boy alternative
26 Walk vainly
29 Supple
31 Refuges
32 Shade of green
34 Greek vowel
35 Caesar, for one
37 Historical period
39 Tree house
40 "__ corny as Kansas . . ."

41 Influence
44 *L.A. Law* actress
45 Man-mouse connector
46 Spewed forth
47 Used the loom again
49 Contented sound
52 Pianist Watts
54 Sales spiel
55 Night noise
58 Actor Baldwin
59 Binding obligation
60 Kentucky fort
62 Desire
63 Stock source: Abbr.
64 Sticky stuff
65 Young-__ (kids)
66 Language suffix

73 PARTING WORDS

by Robert Land

ACROSS

1 Elvis' recording label
4 Pittsburgh player
11 Dolphins' div.
14 ___ de Cologne
15 Synthetic
16 Distant
17 Go astray
18 Parting word
20 Winner over AES
21 Baby kisser
22 Condition
23 Racetrack shape
26 Ayres and Wallace
29 Love god
30 Jane of the jungle
32 They bring joy
34 "___ bragh!"
35 Some entrées
36 *Dungeons & Dragons* publisher
37 Parting word
39 Gal of song
42 Himalayan kingdom
43 Wandering
45 Young hare
48 Drawn up for battle
49 Cassini of fashion
50 Lateen-rigged sailboat
52 Esau's home
53 Scatter
55 Female soldier in WWII
57 ___ de plume
59 Parting words
63 Airline to Tokyo
64 It's next to nothing
65 Swit or Young
66 VCR button
67 Viper's warning
68 World's lowest lake
69 Bat wood

DOWN

1 Yellow fever conqueror
2 Sedan's quartet
3 Parting words
4 Tiny, in Scotland
5 Infield cover
6 Sign up
7 M. Zola
8 Washroom, for short
9 Dutch commune
10 Cincinnati nine
11 Peaked house
12 Contributor
13 Newsmen of old
19 *Les ___-Unis*
24 Former Mideast British colony: Abbr.
25 He stays behind
27 Coach Ewbank
28 Buffy, e.g.
30 "___ the lead out!"
31 Coiled
33 Pied-___
35 CCCX × V
38 Solemn words
39 Parting word
40 Windflowers
41 Inc. cousin
42 Mideast desert
44 "Super!"
45 Both, in Bolivia
46 Singer John et al.
47 Poetic lines
48 Looks forward to
51 Had possession of
54 Frenzied
56 Word form for "cell"
58 Supersonic reading
60 Forest denizen
61 Coach Parseghian
62 High bond rating

74 A LITTLE SEASONING

by Trip Payne

ACROSS

1 Seafood offering
6 Scrooge's shout
9 Flowers holder
13 Lawful
14 Woodchopper's tool
15 Buffalo
16 "__ plan, a canal, . . ."
17 Shrew
19 Annual house chore
21 Wind direction: Abbr.
22 Japanese drama
23 "My __ Sal"
24 It's across the Atl.
25 Actress Moran
27 Health resort
30 School break
34 The wise men
35 Propel a scull
36 Poet Pound
37 End up well, in a way
42 Arid
43 Pseudonyms, for short
44 Wine cask
45 Scale notes
46 Artist Vermeer
47 Actress Wray
50 Shakespeare play
55 Accountants, at tax time
56 Follows stealthily
57 Four-person race
58 Encountered
59 Bert's pal
60 Lampreylike

61 Seals of approval
62 Interest figures

DOWN

1 Social rank
2 Has trouble walking
3 Not __ in the world
4 Maxi's opposite
5 Tin: Lat.
6 Cookie-sheetful
7 Skater's leap
8 At this place
9 Sentry's watch
10 Strong __ ox
11 Composer's output
12 End for depend

15 Cereal fruit
18 Penn and Teller's act
20 Clinton's veep
24 Actor Jannings
25 Linda of *Dynasty*
26 Steak order
27 Measurement
28 Left, on a ship
29 Santa __, CA
30 German valley
31 Like some crowds
32 Hotel unit
33 High-schooler
34 Produced industrially: Abbr.
38 Like many urban streets

39 Private's reply
40 Sky sight
41 Comedian
45 Clear a debt
46 Witticisms
47 Swoon
48 Kate's TV mate
49 Words of approval
50 Birch or elder
51 War, to Sherman
52 Verne captain
53 Difficult journey
54 *Gone With the Wind* manor
55 Prefix meaning "before"

by Fred Piscop

ACROSS

1 Book-jacket copy
6 Dad
10 Nabobs, initially
14 Unearthly
15 New Haven students
16 Novelist Waugh
17 Simple swimming strokes
19 Swamp goo
20 Hydrocarbon suffix
21 Sibelius' "Valse __"
22 "No __, no gain"
23 Potpie veggie
24 Item
26 Spaniel breed
31 Roof covering
32 Carrier to Israel
33 [see other side]
35 Praline morsel
39 Telegram
40 Mailing list items
42 Neuwirth of *Cheers*
43 In sorry shape
45 Wine valley
46 __ breve
47 Iron-pumper's unit
49 Pitcher's dream game
51 Familiar surroundings
55 They're rated in BTUs
56 Tel __
57 African outing
60 Vast expanse
63 Rice wine
64 Bunko business
66 Stadium level
67 Coll. marching group
68 Succotash morsels
69 Reo builder
70 Slangy agreement
71 Have life

DOWN

1 Eliot's *Adam* __
2 Bolshevik Trotsky
3 Egg on
4 Storied sleeper
5 Defeated
6 "Foot" word form
7 "__ fair in love . . ."
8 Michelangelo masterpiece
9 State confidently
10 Flying mammals
11 Of a hipbone
12 Problem for Pauline
13 Public commotion
18 Puff, for one
23 Some heavy machinery
25 Spigot
26 Plies a needle
27 Ballet bend
28 Uncommon
29 Politico Bayh
30 Staff anew
34 Defaulter's loss
36 Gael, for one
37 Up to the job
38 At hand
41 Most of Libya
44 Thus far
48 Bakery offering
50 Stalactite shape
51 Must
52 Be of use
53 Traveled by tandem
54 Sierra Nevada lake
58 Greek salad cheese
59 St. Louis landmark
60 Teamster's rig
61 Hellenic H's
62 Mgr.'s helper
65 Kids' cereal

76 FOR THE TAKING

by Rich Norris

ACROSS

1 Pub missile
5 Of bad character
9 __ fatale
14 In excess of
15 Paddy product
16 Beelike
17 Sandwich shop
18 English river
19 Nearly even, as a race
20 Have lunch on the run
23 __ Park, CO
24 Moon lander
25 Mao __-tung
28 Poor grade
29 Chuck wagon meal
33 Soundness of mind
35 Ivories tickler
37 Whodunit game
38 What *carpe diem* means
40 Sore feeling
42 Oregon city
43 Casino employee
45 "__ Cassius has a lean . . ."
46 Map lines: Abbr.
49 Reading room
50 AMA members
52 Surf droplets
54 Get desperate
59 Iranian faith
61 At the summit of
62 __ time (never)
63 Advantage
64 Author Jaffe
65 Thought-provoking
66 They hold your horses
67 Give off
68 Vegas calculation

DOWN

1 Evaded, as questions
2 Reluctant
3 Give an account of
4 Native American group
5 Important times
6 __ *Las Vegas*
7 Screen image
8 Ivan of tennis
9 Daughter of Muhammad
10 Larger-than-life
11 With great strength
12 __-jongg
13 Tolkien tree giant
21 Computer-data format
22 Shoot-'em-up
26 Actor Irwin
27 CBS logo
30 Golfers' obstacles
31 Change for a five
32 Quick with one-liners
34 Final Four org.
35 Fruit covering
36 Chaser's word
38 China's largest city
39 Performed, biblically
40 Tack on
41 Fair grade
44 Hits the "send" button
46 Containing violence, maybe
47 Became apparent to, with "on"
48 Web site workers
51 Trunk contents
53 Madrid museum
55 Drops from the sky
56 Tiny particle
57 Nobelist Morrison
58 Disagreement
59 Gymnastics device
60 Ciao, to Caesar

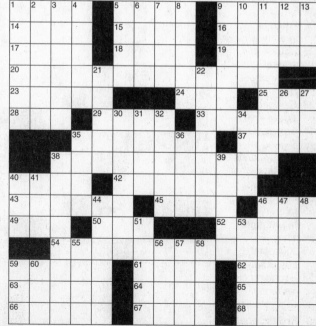

by Bob Lubbers

ACROSS

1 Harper Valley org.
4 Squalls
10 Canonized *femme*: Abbr.
13 Capek drama
14 Military leg-wraps
16 Heavy weight
17 Sphere
18 Reception device
19 Louvre fare
20 New York Indians
22 Chaney, Sr. or Jr.
23 Rocky ridge
24 Overstuff
25 He played McHale
27 Boxer, slangily
31 Bit
32 Try to hit, as a fly
35 Square or granny
36 '30s actress Helen
39 Railroad siding
41 Apia resident
42 Sea eagle
43 Current units
47 Onetime poet laureate
51 Sax range
53 Literary monogram
54 They: Fr.
55 *Kidnapped* character
58 Shocking swimmer
59 Old gold coin of Spain
61 Mount in Crete
62 French summer
63 Abu Dhabi, e.g.
64 Part of RSVP
65 Latvia, once: Abbr.
66 Two-__ (kind of car)
67 Dawn goddess

DOWN

1 Gumshoe's quest
2 Rutabaga, for one
3 Where Alexander defeated Darius
4 WWI French plane
5 Game fish
6 Mel et al.
7 66 or I-95
8 __ Park, NJ
9 Spanish gent
10 Depots
11 CN Tower city
12 Petition to
15 Warbled
21 Feeling poorly
25 Jason or Justine
26 Puma rival
28 Full of: Suff.
29 Rice athletes
30 Polynesian beverage
33 Molecule part
34 Golf hazard
36 Mole, for one
37 Small songbird
38 Wind dir.
39 Couches
40 Appliance timesavers
44 Brit. fliers
45 Plaza Hotel brat
46 Small apartment
48 "Oh no!"
49 Some slacks
50 Actor Davis
52 Grad school rituals
55 Vessel
56 __ Oder (German river)
57 Impolite look
60 __ la la

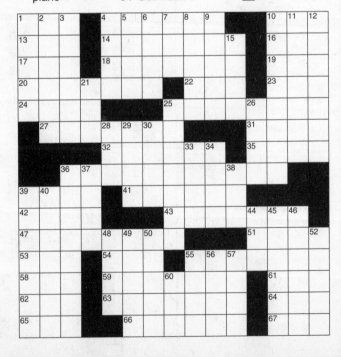

by A.J. Santora

ACROSS

1 Tarzan's mate
5 1990 World Series winners
9 Powder
13 Imitative
15 This and that
16 Hebrew month
17 Start of a Mae West film quote
19 Biblical mount
20 Part 2 of quote
22 Suez Canal terminus
23 Squash variety
24 Harmful fly
27 Collective suffix
29 Admit
30 Depiction
35 Passing fancy
36 Part 3 of quote
38 Andrea __ Sarto
39 No longer jammed
41 Joined
42 Zeno's home
43 Like some angels
46 Choreography units
49 Saltworks
52 Part 4 of quote
56 Caesarean phrase
57 End of quote
59 Schönberg's *Moses und __*
60 Annealing oven
61 Best
62 Green vegetable
63 Commotions
64 Play first

DOWN

1 __ alai
2 Each
3 Boy, in Barcelona
4 Go with
5 Pathways
6 Elmer's partner
7 Scorned
8 Before too long
9 Freight train unit
10 Glandular word form
11 Repair cost
12 Watch knob
14 "__ Johnny!"
18 Broadly
21 1800s Chief Justice
24 Bean curd
25 Gottfried, in *Lohengrin*
26 Means justifiers
28 Naval off.
30 Roped again
31 Before
32 Hero
33 Hawaiian bird
34 __ plaid
36 Director Raoul
37 Otho's realm: Abbr.
40 Planet discovered in 1846
43 Sawyer's pal
44 Touch-__ (risky)
45 Aboveboard
46 Gridiron play
47 Fish in a bowl
48 Praise to the sky
50 Unit of conductance
51 Leo's dens
53 Bruins' sch.
54 *"Vissi d'__"*
55 Soft drink
58 Up-to-date, for short

VALENTINE GIFTS

by Lee Weaver

ACROSS

1 British racecourse
6 Automotive giant: Abbr.
9 Ego
13 More sad
14 Small brook
16 Brainstorm
17 Dried coconut
18 Jai __
19 Dutch cheese
20 "*Agnus __*"
21 Bright fabric pattern
24 Resided
26 Uncovers
27 Fixate
29 Plant life
31 Barbecue offerings
32 Hamburger toppers
34 Trumped-up story
37 Ink spots
39 Ancient
40 Computer symbols
42 Put in stitches
43 Veal meal
46 Shakespeare's river
47 Window units
48 Ancient ascetic
50 Turn aside
52 Mrs. Gorbachev
53 '60s hippie
56 Noncommercial TV network: Abbr.
59 *Café au __*
60 River of Russia
61 Bounds along easily
63 Author Gardner
64 Smooth the way
65 Social radiance
66 Part of U.S.A.
67 For what reason
68 Flower parts

DOWN

1 Start of a nursery-school song
2 __ gin fizz
3 Mythical arrow shooter
4 Above, in verse
5 Negligible amounts
6 Civil War general
7 Temperate
8 Potter's material
9 __ Leone
10 Cantor of vaudeville
11 Pounces (upon)
12 Public regard
15 Capital of Portugal
22 And
23 Foot bones
25 Compass direction
27 Spheres
28 Peevish temper
29 Satiates
30 Gold deposit
33 Memo
34 Tomato
35 Get __ the ground floor
36 Anglo-Saxon laborer
38 Frighten
41 Mama __ Elliot
44 Erroneous
45 Freshwater duck
47 Tin/lead alloy
49 Moves furtively
50 Frighten
51 Curtain fabric
52 Life of __ (ease)
53 Dog's irritant
54 Chicken's gullet
55 Leftovers dish
57 Ray of light
58 Onetime Orly arrivals: Abbr.
62 Halloween mo.

80 LOW-IMPACT EXERCISE

by Norma Steinberg

ACROSS

1 Wide ties
7 Universal Studios' former parent
10 Actress Basinger
13 Nova __
14 Put in order
16 Scaling the hierarchy
18 Lifeboats
19 Golfer's props
20 Ike's command: Abbr.
21 Susan of *L.A. Law*
22 Flower site
23 Four-footed friend
25 __ Speedwagon
28 Charity performance
30 Housekeeper
31 Bit of land
33 Pig __ poke
34 *Bus Stop* playwright
35 Working without a break, maybe
39 Picks up the check
40 Unified
41 Bird food ingredient
42 Dutch painter
43 Tough situations
46 Here: Fr.
47 Architect I.M. __
48 Pot cover
49 Quantity: Abbr.
52 "Wow!"
54 College official
56 Butter alternative
57 Remote control activity
60 Reaches
61 Actress __ Sue Martin
62 Author's submissions: Abbr.
63 School org.
64 Shorthand specialists

DOWN

1 Syrian leader
2 Cross the goal line
3 Arrogant
4 Singer Redding
5 Spanish aunt
6 *Bambi* author
7 Tom, Dick, or Harry
8 Making brittle
9 Supply weapons to
10 Make booties
11 Unawareness
12 Actress Ryan
15 Help with a heist
17 Yield
22 Roadrunner's cry
24 Etc. relative
26 Number of sides on stop signs
27 Keatsian output
28 Ecstasy
29 Of higher quality
30 Less
31 Jacob's father
32 Ceiling features
36 Stance
37 Episode
38 Secondhand
39 __ Beta Kappa
44 "Too bad!"
45 Locker photos
47 Clinton cabinet apppointee
49 Strange
50 The Wizard of __ Park
51 Roman robes
53 Victuals
55 *Born Free* lioness
56 "All __" (Porter tune)
57 Machine part
58 Tiny bite
59 Snitch

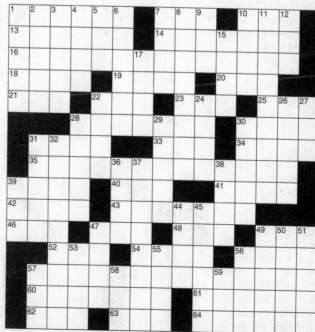

ACROSS

1 Dole's '96 running mate
5 Top of the head
10 Yen
14 Pelvic bones
15 Tsar, for one
16 Words after fa
17 1949 Literature Nobelist
20 Ran without moving
21 Green Gables girl
22 Obtained
23 Congressional unit
26 __ off (sore)
28 1993 Literature Nobelist
33 Liable
36 Role for Lorre
37 Busybody
38 Pianist Peter
40 Network filler
43 Eve's opposite
44 Vacation jaunts
46 Haven't __ to stand on
48 It may scare you
49 1936 Literature Nobelist
53 Void's partner
54 Son of Aaron
58 Mile High Center architect
61 Auction actions
63 Appetite stimulus
64 1954 Literature Nobelist
68 It often comes with a proposal
69 Like some seals
70 "__ kleine Nachtmusik"
71 Mexican moola
72 Male deers
73 Leafed through

DOWN

1 New Zealand birds
2 Omit in pronunciation
3 Paper producers
4 Most wan
5 Sp. lady
6 Magna __ laude
7 A, in communications
8 Primitive shelter
9 Gardener, at times
10 Type
11 Distinctive flavor
12 Singer Laine
13 Poet Crane
18 Translator's challenge
19 Suspicious
24 __ about
25 Late hours, informally
27 Per __ (daily)
29 Happy Days actress
30 Nose-in-the-air type
31 Another: Sp.
32 Prefix for second
33 Start a pot
34 Land of the Incas
35 Math subject
39 Word on a store sign
41 1997 Peter Fonda role
42 Diamond of note
45 Ignores disdainfully
47 Gather with effort
50 Special groups
51 Out-of-date
52 Not as little
55 "Yikes!"
56 Iowa commune
57 Like the sun, in some photos
58 Cop's quarry
59 Albany's canal
60 Wayside havens
62 Flu fighters
65 Swelled head
66 One of the March women
67 Bouncer's requests

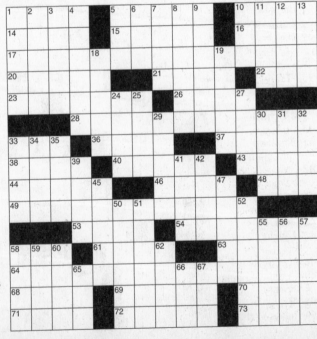

T PARTY

by S.E. Booker

ACROSS

1 Tabula __
5 Train tracks
10 Trevi tosser's thought
14 Troop truant
15 Turn topsy-turvy
16 Topical treatment
17 Trey's trefoil
18 Torment
19 Toe the __
20 Torquemada's territory
22 Trickery
24 Taxis
26 Truckee town
27 Tumbler
30 Tailors
33 Toast
34 Taunt
36 Tatter
38 Tokyo, to Takeshita
39 Tax tribulation
41 Temerity
42 Telepathy
43 Tyrant's title
44 Together, to Toscanini
45 Turn tail
49 Trustfulness
51 Tall-tale teller
52 Tucker
53 Terrifying
55 Tintinnabulated
59 Thailand
60 Thirst tamers
64 Twisted together
65 Too
66 Tie
67 *Tosca* tune
68 Transactor
69 Typesetter's text
70 Talk tempestuously

DOWN

1 Tear
2 Tannery tools
3 __ tureen
4 Tuna type
5 Turnip
6 Thug
7 "This __ test"
8 The, to Thérèse
9 Tipsy
10 Thrash
11 Tennis troublemaker
12 TV threesome
13 Tee tail?
21 Trap
23 Tempest __ teapot
25 Thicker through the tummy
26 Twinkling
27 Tylenol target
28 Took
29 Turnpike turnoffs
31 Traffic
32 Tours toast
35 Tabloids take them
37 Transport
40 Tramps
41 Tattled
46 Tumult
47 Televise
48 Tends to the tab
50 Temper
53 Tiller's tower
54 Tec's task
56 Traditional tales
57 Turpitude
58 Transaction
59 Tearful
61 __ tear
62 Tunnel (through)
63 Took tiffin

83 A DAY AT THE RACES

by Fred Piscop

ACROSS
1 Vanzetti's partner
6 Rugged rock
10 Cummerbund
14 Actor Delon
15 Man Friday
16 Utah ski resort
17 Three races
20 Flamboyant pianist
21 "Uncle!"
22 Actress Lenska
23 Pharaoh in *The Ten Commandments*
25 Available to let
28 Rival of Hingis
29 Comic Sandler
30 Whatsoever
31 Barker and Kettle
34 Three races
38 Med. specialty
39 Sultan's group
40 Add to staff
41 Actor Burton
42 Talked on and on and on . . .
44 Benin, once
47 Pro-shop bagful
48 "There __ atheists . . ."
49 Sanitation crew pickup
53 Three races
56 Barry or Brubeck
57 Rake
58 Vidalia or Bermuda
59 North Sea feeder
60 Two-__ sloth
61 MTV fans

DOWN
1 Humorist Mort
2 Jai __
3 Auto part, for short
4 Wide-screen movie process
5 Close, as a ball game
6 Brutus colleague
7 Teeming
8 Commotion
9 Terra- relative
10 Snorkel and others
11 Schwarzenegger's middle name
12 Barrel strip
13 Where the Styx flows

18 Pretzel topper
19 Opportune
23 Domain
24 __ breve
25 Urn
26 Yemeni port
27 Defeatist's word
28 Beef on the hoof
30 Orderly grouping
31 Common street name
32 Realty unit
33 Depot posting, for short
35 Organized crime
36 Roof edge
37 Western tribe
41 More drawn-out

42 Piece of business
43 Filmed over
44 Mary Martin song subject
45 Tapestry
46 Ho's companion
47 Trapped, in a way
49 Like a deadeye's aim
50 Mold-ripened cheese
51 "Well, I'll be __ of a gun!"
52 USAF honchos
54 Uffizi display
55 Milne marsupial

84 LET'S RIDE

by Rich Norris

ACROSS

1 Arthur of tennis
5 Blockhead
9 Blasé
14 Reiser or Revere
15 Sandwich cookie
16 Fine wood
17 Leaves
19 "Drink to me only with __ eyes . . ."
20 Available, as a physician
21 With 52 Across, leaves
23 Slangy turndown
24 Allow
26 Anthem preposition
27 Becomes indistinct
30 Blithe
33 Aerosol output
36 Seagoing: Abbr.
37 Southwestern stewpot
38 Leaves
41 Charitable offerings
42 Fast horse
43 Mideast country
44 Aware, slangily
45 Weapons to launch
47 Raft implement
48 "Agnus __"
49 *The Simpsons* grocery owner
52 See 21 Across
57 "The Duke of Brooklyn"
59 Sign up
60 Leaves
62 British length measure
63 Donated
64 Sound of music
65 Fresh-mouthed
66 Comedian Laurel
67 "__ Death" (Grieg work)

DOWN

1 Cook's garb
2 Steam bath
3 Intuition
4 Actress Lanchester
5 Gussied (up)
6 Spanish gold
7 Camera part
8 Loose garment
9 Fashionable crowd
10 Dislike intensely
11 Slay
12 Feminine ending
13 Prepares Easter eggs
18 Puts to rest, as fear
22 Lad
25 Pavarotti et al.
27 Short-lived fashions
28 Gilbert and Teasdale
29 Offer more than, at auction
30 Rip off
31 Shaving-cream ingredient
32 Tall tale
33 Former Iranian monarch
34 Brazilian soccer great
35 Freeway access
37 Shelley works
39 Tinkerbell, for one
40 Keeping tabs on
45 Comic Moms __
46 Abate
47 Aromas
49 Sayonara, in Spain
50 Tubular pasta
51 Strongly suggests
52 Jeweler's inventory
53 Draft rating
54 Food morsels
55 Quiche needs
56 Pants part
58 Microscopic amount
61 Dam-building agcy.

85 LET'S RIDE

by Lee Weaver

ACROSS

1 Energy choice
6 Alan of *M*A*S*H*
10 "I taut I __ a puddy tat!"
13 Make amends
14 Exercise, as power
16 Fire residue
17 *Diagnosis Murder* star
19 Roman dozen
20 Squared building stones
21 Wee tree
23 Shade tree
24 Heavy burden
25 Fix a pillow, perhaps
29 Weather term
32 Bullring "Bravo!"
33 Swiss mathematician
35 Doctrine
36 Verdi heroine
38 Cantered
40 *The Lion King* villain
41 Data, for short
43 Long-necked lute
45 Summer, in Lyon
46 Lease signers
48 Forehead neighbor
50 As the __ flies
51 School zone sign
52 Placed back on the payroll
55 Docking fee
59 Important time
60 Vegetable grower
62 French friend
63 Bowler's headache
64 "__ is an island . . ."
65 Cause damage to
66 Smelting residue
67 Declared by oath

DOWN

1 Actress Thompson
2 Elevator inventor
3 Lake, in Scotland
4 Hosiery item
5 Assess again
6 Barley beards
7 Container cover
8 Former Algerian officials
9 Acid's opposite
10 Ballroom employee
11 T __ "Tom"
12 Tory's opponent
15 Expel from a country
18 Load of wood
22 Gold fabrics
25 Banquet with barbs
26 Superior group
27 Vehicle of yore
28 Dentist's instruction
29 Mountain ridge
30 Former defense grp.
31 Scatter
34 Prefix for center
37 Video game name
39 __ *Wine and Roses*
42 Derisive sounds
44 Lets have again
47 Insignificant fellows
49 Take temporarily
52 Paper measure
53 Humorist Bombeck
54 Not sharp
55 Science of selling: Abbr.
56 Snowballs, sometimes
57 Equipment
58 Sea eagle
61 Spy org.

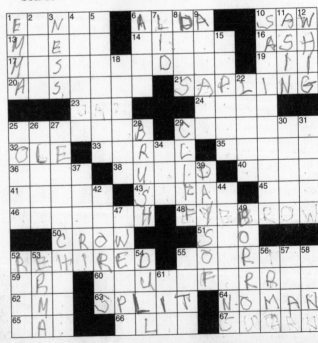

by Bob Lubbers

ACROSS

1 Singer Yma
6 Flowery garlands
10 *Citizen Kane* prop
14 BP acquisition
15 Mayberry sheriff
16 Smidgen
17 Western spread
18 Evade, with "of"
20 Retains
22 *The Jazz Singer*, e.g.
23 Apathy
25 Vigoda and Fortas
27 LBJ aide
28 Keep in mind
33 Tarzan creator's initials
34 Refined iron
36 Gene Tierney title role
37 Gene components
39 Firefighter Red
41 Economist Greenspan
42 Indonesian island
44 Nerd
46 WWII vessel
47 Korea, Japan, etc.
49 River through Toledo
51 "__ went thataway!"
52 Odin's home
53 "__ *Fideles*"
57 Flower-petal oil
58 Euphoria
61 Signed
64 Sunburn soother
65 Take five
66 "__ Billy Joe"
67 Mrs. Truman
68 Hardens
69 Hoopster Archibald et al.

DOWN

1 Patriotic org.
2 Actress Thurman
3 Playground fixture
4 Agree (to)
5 Some beneficiaries
6 Statutes
7 Chemical suffix
8 Neighbor of Mont.
9 Gambler's method
10 Window adjunct
11 "__ who's talking!"
12 Tweezer case
13 Dinner companion
19 Studio tripod
21 *Ristorante* course
23 Punish by fine
24 Eye part
25 Basement entrance
26 Contradict
29 Meadow sound
30 Stock-price elevator
31 Pencil tip
32 Blew one's top
35 Rickenbacker or Murphy
38 Posed
40 Frame a photo again
43 Dull finish
45 Fort
48 Clippers
50 African nation
53 *Pequod* master
54 Former Red Cross head
55 Hollywood clashers
56 __ *Gotta Have It* (Spike Lee film)
57 Hill builders
59 Churchillian sign
60 Superlative suffix
62 French season
63 John __ Passos

DOGGONE IT

by Fred Piscop

ACROSS

1 Grab all of
4 Sank, as a putt
9 __ voce
14 Festive night, often
15 Vestment
16 Studied, with "over"
17 Canine actor?
19 Sky shade
20 __-ran
21 How a sponge may live
23 Counterculture guru
25 *"Mangia!"*
26 Friend, in the 'hood
29 Mills' locales
33 He'll suit you
35 Sees eye to eye
37 Hosiery shade
38 Canine invaders?
42 Painter Chagall
43 Conical abode
44 *Pogo* alligator
47 Kind of wrench
50 Canadian prov.
51 Corn serving
53 Nickeled and __
55 Jockey Ron
60 White House staffer
61 Cathedral topper
63 Canine actor?
65 Nation east of Fiji
66 Strike-zone boundary
67 Holm or McKellen
68 Barely defeated
69 Composer Saint-__
70 Corrida shout

DOWN

1 Of the blood
2 Rudimentary seeds
3 Insinuates
4 Used to own
5 Actor Epps
6 Club-soda garnish
7 MBA subj.
8 Al __ (pasta order)
9 Peloponnesian War victor
10 Move like the Blob
11 Unwaveringly staunch
12 Three times, to a druggist
13 Praiseful poem
18 City near Los Angeles
22 Diet component
24 Safecracker
27 Curtain holders
28 Blast-furnace input
30 SFO posting
31 Shake hands with
32 Palindromic tennis pro
34 Not facing the truth
36 Name for a herd dog
38 Gander or bull
39 Traveling a la the ISS
40 __-Locka, FL
41 Tear apart
42 Triple-A handout
45 Take a second look at
46 Center X
48 Actor Estevez
49 Start a new hand
52 Ice, in bar lingo
54 Colonial patriot Silas
56 Craving
57 Sandwich filler
58 Genealogy diagram
59 Perfect place
61 Sault __ Marie
62 Peas' place
64 Battleship letters

by A.J. Santora

ACROSS

1 Loses control
6 City west of Sparks
10 Summer coolers
14 __ Rogers St. Johns
15 Airline to Lod
16 Barrie dog
17 Pitcher Ryan
18 Rommel's nickname
20 SUV model
22 Auction finish
23 Old hand
24 Coming next
27 Unruly ones
31 Fractional prefix
32 For one
34 Tennessee team
36 MTV toon
37 Western capital
41 Dory mover
42 Stage strap
43 Odious one
44 Avoid
46 Include
49 Satie et al.
51 Scale notes
52 Deadlock
55 NFL team
60 Florida State team
62 Greek gelt
63 Pistol, so to speak
64 Soccer great
65 Atlas rocket
66 Sharpness
67 Way out
68 *Sometimes a Great Notion* author

DOWN

1 Cover ground
2 Like a lot
3 Of the soft palate
4 Panache
5 Shore bird
6 Cinnamon candy
7 "Waitin' for the Robert __"
8 CNN reporter Octavia
9 Sticks at the market
10 Mean
11 School adjunct
12 Rock producer Brian
13 Mellow instrument
19 Onetime rival of MGM
21 __-Magnon
25 Change
26 Engine knock
27 Singer Orbison
28 Newsreel segment
29 To-do
30 Foxy
32 By __ (barely)
33 Fruit tree
35 In a way
37 Approach
38 "__ Blu Dipinto Di Blu"
39 Actress Peeples
40 French pronoun
45 On the slopes
47 Pantry feature
48 Roach of Hollywood
50 Japanese honorific
52 Golf-cart foursome
53 __ fell swoop
54 Attempt
56 Sulk
57 Holly tree
58 Grinder shop
59 Mammoth
60 Ride the bench
61 Gaslight, e.g.

89 GO ON AHEAD

by Norma Steinberg

ACROSS

1 Drains
5 Linguini or penne
10 TV clown
14 Grand Ole __
15 Exhausted
16 Zealous
17 Elvis __ Presley
18 Byways
19 She preceded Ashcroft
20 Barbecue bit
21 Charismatic, in 1999
23 Mottos
25 Flightless bird
26 Desire
27 Percussion instruments
32 Outlaw Starr
34 Have children, biblically
35 Historical period
36 Vicinity
37 Spoke softly
38 So-so
39 Term of respect
40 Gusts of air
41 Tokyo district
42 Revolutionary War soldiers
44 Rani's dress
45 Sportscaster Cross
46 Filters
49 Budgetary limit
54 Smidgen
55 Basil or rosemary
56 Reef material
57 Undulating
58 Opera solo
59 French river
60 Cain's brother
61 Repair
62 All done
63 "Auld Lang __"

DOWN

1 Skyrockets
2 Showery month
3 They strike for money
4 Opp. of ant.
5 Mom or pop
6 Then, in Paris
7 Thick slice
8 Shipshape
9 Talked back
10 American showman
11 Roast cooker
12 Fans' publication
13 Smell
21 Copenhagen native
22 Fake: Abbr.
24 Festive
27 Feline sounds
28 Ripens
29 Kid's collectible
30 McCain's home state: Abbr.
31 Actress Gilbert
32 Big party
33 Cleveland's water
34 Blessing
37 Shoulder bone
38 Caveman discovery
40 Finch or dove
41 Robin Williams film role
43 Mythical sailor
44 Climbed
46 Alarm
47 *Separate Tables* star
48 Panache
49 Pillow covering
50 Father: Fr.
51 Ireland
52 Lunchtime for some
53 Cross-hatched design
57 Used to be

ACROSS

1 Satisfy, as a debt
6 Dieter's limitations
10 Influence unfairly
14 Solo
15 *Siete* follower
16 Concerning
17 Wealthy
19 Recipe instruction
20 Lower school: Abbr.
21 Singer Rimes
22 Tall-hat wearer
23 Gone by
25 Narrative continuations
27 Of lesser status
32 Barbershop order
33 Presidential nickname
34 Doled (out)
36 *Uncle Tom's Cabin* author
39 Wire measures
41 Rescued
43 Impediment
44 Nabbed morays
46 Biblical peak
48 Unit of energy
49 Managed-care grps.
51 Thesaurus entries
53 Horse-drawn vehicles
56 Once __ while
57 Hammer part
58 "No bid," in bridge

61 __ *Window* (Hitchcock film)
65 *Damn Yankees* vamp
66 Wealthy
68 Utter confidently
69 Head: Fr.
70 Blakley of *Nashville*
71 In order
72 Swine's supper
73 Stockholm resident

DOWN

1 Hard to find
2 Israeli airline
3 Jab playfully
4 Twenty Questions category
5 Kobe currency
6 Pâté de __ gras
7 Official proceedings
8 Dilutes
9 14-line poem
10 Bakery products
11 Wealthy
12 Shakespearean spirit
13 Manor workers
18 Hand warmers
24 Ruby, for one
26 P-T connection
27 Weak, as an excuse
28 Tony relative
29 Wealthy
30 Greek letters
31 Wrangler rivals
35 Reject as false
37 Balmy
38 Bacon partner
40 Future minister's school
42 Breakfast pastry
45 Popular pet
47 Gas particle
50 Work periods
52 Tightly defined
53 Water-balloon impact sound
54 10th-century pope
55 Sales pitch
59 Choir voice
60 Short distance
62 German article
63 Served perfectly
64 '50s South Korean president
67 Decade units: Abbr.

by Bob Lubbers

ACROSS

1 Cads
6 Two-bagger: Abbr.
9 Attempts
14 __ of roses
15 Epoch
16 Annoy
17 Sci-fi velocity
19 Wield rubber
20 Proofer's word
21 Clean-air org.
22 Frisky feline
23 Monsters
25 "__ Clear Day . . ."
26 Faction
31 Cool it
33 Regrettable
34 "What __ is new?"
35 Have title to
36 Penpoint
39 Comedienne Charlotte
41 Hideaway
42 NBA team
44 Narc's org.
46 Lean-tos
48 Crop bin
52 Teachers' grp.
53 Star in Cygnus
54 __ With Wolves
57 Hostelry
58 Nag nibbles
62 Made stringed potatoes
63 Fisherman's tie
65 Worship
66 Sleep phenomenon: Abbr.
67 Oscar de la __
68 Founded (upon)
69 Balaam's beast
70 Villainous glare

DOWN

1 Hems and __
2 French state
3 Raison d'__
4 Portable PCs
5 Next year's alums: Abbr.
6 Intensify
7 Chicken parts
8 Dog of fiction
9 Involved with
10 Steak style
11 Rat-__
12 Foundation
13 British machine gun
18 Persian fairy
22 Director Sir Alexander
24 Secluded valley
26 __ Ana, CA
27 Jug handle
28 More mature
29 Previously owned
30 Writes
31 Viet __
32 Water pitcher
37 Brainstorms
38 Barbara __ Geddes
40 Ferrara noble name
43 Forthright
45 Roman magistrates
47 Sinatra's hometown
49 Necessitated
50 Snake poisons
51 Part of AD
54 Part of OD
55 Verdi opera
56 Sgts., e.g.
59 Name of two of Henry's six
60 Lug
61 Headliner
63 Bikini part
64 AMA members

92 PARTY LINES

by Robert Land

ACROSS

1 Berth place
5 Hay cube
9 Wine barrel
13 Author Ferber
14 Give cheer to
16 Tag on some quotes
17 Party line
20 For example
21 From way off
22 Kay Thompson heroine
23 Brew, in Bavaria
24 __ instant (quickly)
25 Dewey's uncle
28 "There's __ in the air"
29 Tenderfoot's org.
32 Wally of cookiedom
33 Leo and Libra
34 Handy bit of Latin
35 Party line
39 Freud subject
40 Make into law
41 Give kudos
42 __ Simeon (Hearst Castle site)
43 Overhead curve
44 Maintains the shrubbery
46 Small cart
47 Camembert kin
48 Where a bug is snug
51 See 38 Down
52 NASA affirmative
55 Party line
58 King of Norway
59 Signor Alighieri
60 Actor Ladd
61 Brain part
62 Dandelion, e.g.
63 Greek entree

DOWN

1 Church seating
2 Creative spur
3 That green feeling
4 *Norma* __
5 Put up a fuss
6 Rite place
7 Comic actor Bert
8 Airport stat.
9 Konica competitor
10 Contra- relative
11 Porcine mamas
12 Where a sock may reach
15 Dinner time
18 Daily delivery
19 Go by
23 Striped swimmer
24 Goody for Goldfinger
25 Evans and Carnegie
26 Psi follower
27 Preempted, perhaps
28 Capital of Hawaii?
29 Playwright Brendan
30 Canyon of the comics
31 Forest units
33 Actor Keach
36 Prepare for action
37 Apt anagram for "angered"
38 With 51 Across, John Wayne's Oscar film
44 Tagged in the store
45 Actress Moreno
46 Motored
47 No gentleman
48 One adored
49 __ contendere
50 "__ the Arab" (Ray Stevens song)
51 Vanished
52 Comrade in arms
53 Actor Sharif
54 Casino offering
56 Course deviation
57 Time delay

93 EASY DOES IT

by A.J. Santora

ACROSS

1 Savory jelly
6 Taste
9 Complains
14 Wingless stage
15 Veteran
16 Irish Rebellion hero
17 Climbing plants
19 French narrative
20 Door openers
22 Do numbers
25 Final ender
26 Ready replacement
27 Dakota Indian
28 Raisin center
30 Small drums
32 Albacore
33 Lawrence portrayer
36 Ukulele phrase
41 Lack of vigor
42 Envelope closer
44 Bed canopy
47 "Thanatopsis" poet
49 Leftover tidbit
50 Spanish Mrs.
52 Mauna __
53 Area code 208: Abbr.
54 Polite request
58 John Le __
59 Shooter's order
63 Enjoyed
64 Ambulance fig.
65 Eliminate
66 Work agenda
67 Get the picture
68 More mad

DOWN

1 Capp and Capone
2 Adage
3 Post- opposite
4 "The Unanswered Question" composer
5 Marsh plant
6 Wheat used for livestock feed
7 "Dies __"
8 Stations
9 Unsophisticated
10 Out of control
11 TV's Joker
12 Function of some wheels
13 Has a funny feeling
18 Pedro's pelf
21 Lacking
22 Ship direction
23 Oil barrel
24 Dispute
29 1978 Nobel sharer
31 Thickset
33 German physicist
34 __-Pan (Clavell novel)
35 She-bear: Sp.
37 Ballroom dances
38 Madison's veep
39 Jai __
40 Dudevant's nom de plume
43 Sch. group
44 '60s TV toon
45 Correction list
46 Cubic meters
47 Airline's former name
48 Spates
51 Church areas
52 WWII island
55 WWII island
56 Unconvincing
57 Architect Saarinen
60 Pitcher gripper
61 Wind dir.
62 Poet's adverb

ACROSS

1 Free ticket
5 "__ I care!"
9 French cleric
13 Share a border with
14 Wonderland visitor
15 Daily delivery
16 City in *Italia*
17 Return quickly
19 Cuban dances
21 Mexican mister
22 "I cannot __ lie"
23 Fame
26 Sends in payment
29 Injury
31 Football scores: Abbr.
33 Skiing spot
35 Division word
36 Soaks with water
38 Shoulder wrap
40 Suit to __
41 Melville novel
42 Code of conduct
44 Asner and Bradley
45 South American sport
48 She says "Alas!"
50 Took to the ice
52 Yard enclosure
54 Olympic sleds
56 Rotates rapidly
58 Get to know, by chance
62 Endure
63 Busy as __
64 Sponsorship
65 TV host Jay
66 Babysit
67 Singer Loretta
68 Draws to a close

DOWN

1 Young salmon
2 Approximately
3 Certain theater productions
4 Unchanging
5 High mountain
6 Knights' titles
7 More chilly
8 Parsley family member
9 Food of the gods
10 Ram's remark
11 Paper Mate rival
12 Type of deer
14 Attacks vigorously
18 Auctioneer's last word
20 Charitable offering
24 Liniment scent
25 Made a memo
27 Carry
28 Dalmatian markings
30 Negative votes
31 "Terrible" age stage
32 Audition tapes
34 K-12 school designation
37 Designated thus
39 Pizza fractions, often
43 Gnaw
46 Decorative case
47 Pertaining to a king's rule
49 Safe to consume
51 Donald Duck nephew
53 African antelope
55 Omen
57 Signs at big hits
58 Jack Sprat's bane
59 Lincoln's nickname
60 Thriller author Deighton
61 Sardines holder

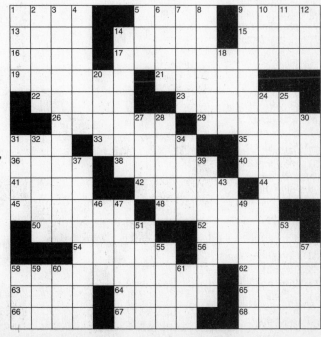

95 ORDER IN THE COURT

by Rich Norris

ACROSS

1 Just __ (slightly)
5 Rodeo rope
11 New Deal monogram
14 Truck-stop stopper
15 Storm surf, vis-à-vis a beachfront
16 Actor Stephen
17 Social worker's file
19 Yet, in poems
20 Cause a chuckle
21 1952 Winter Olympics site
22 Energy
23 According to
24 Gents
26 Went temporarily off course
28 Jeans fabric
30 Golden-coated steed
33 Letter-bottom abbr.
34 Party times
35 Grant permission to
36 *Beverly Hills Cop* actor
40 Burger holder
41 Pay period, perhaps
42 Baking container
43 Salad fruits
45 "Do __ a Waltz?"
48 Satisfy, as a debt
49 Three-time heavyweight champ
50 Director Craven
52 Unused
53 Favoritism
56 Breakfast order
58 Sewing-basket item
59 Dugout chatterbox
61 Pub selection
62 Bowman
63 Greenish blue
64 Hitched, so to speak
65 Tension
66 Poker payment

DOWN

1 Songwriters' grp.
2 Smiled broadly
3 "There's no doubt in my mind!"
4 Links
5 Waikiki welcome
6 Fiery crime
7 Spoils
8 Pop star, e.g.
9 Pertaining to planes
10 Give it a go
11 Human spontaneity
12 Grew, as friendship
13 Was in charge of
18 *To Have and Have Not* author
22 Shriver of tennis
25 Hosted
26 WWI Japanese emperor
27 i topper
29 Actor Beatty
30 Looks prematurely, perhaps
31 "Bird" word form
32 Soup legume
36 Youngster
37 Sealed, say
38 Classic car
39 Unified
40 Candy purchase
44 Crow's cry
46 Get up
47 Find another table for
49 *Angela's* __
51 Distinctive manner
53 Former Miss America host Parks
54 Rise: Abbr.
55 Tummy trouble
57 Numerical prefix
58 Rabbit's foot
59 __-relief
60 PSAT takers

96 GO, TEAM, GO

by Fred Piscop

ACROSS

1 Prom partner
5 Bondsmen
10 Carrier to Ben Gurion Airport
14 Slanted type: Abbr.
15 Fast on one's feet
16 Be in accord
17 Air conditioner alternative
19 Black, as piano keys
20 Innate gift
21 Act the siren
23 GI morale booster
24 Center X
26 Toss about
29 Less significant
31 James __ Garfield
35 Wood chopper
36 Beast with three-pointed antlers
38 Served well
39 Jump-start necessity
42 Preserves, perhaps
43 Poe's "__ Lee"
44 Gulped down
45 __ Park, CO
46 Inlay material
50 Commuter's headache
52 One "T" in TNT
54 Superman foe Luthor
55 When mammoths roamed
59 Where telecommuters work
61 Companion of Dick and Spot
63 Pipe-cleaning company
65 Walkie-talkie punctuation
66 Champion's claim
67 Sharpen
68 Critical witticism
69 Villainous look
70 "Shall we?" response

DOWN

1 Formal declaration
2 Relaxed
3 Custom-make
4 *Vogue* rival
5 Year-end temp
6 Quiche need
7 Widespread
8 Custard treat
9 Shipped out
10 VCR button
11 "Mr. Showmanship"
12 Blood-type group
13 Quarterback Dawson
18 Emcee's openers
22 Belief
25 Rhythmic
27 Former mates
28 Take the plunge
30 Bow-toting god
32 City on the Aare
33 Find new actors for
34 Subject of Ibn Saud
37 JFK postings
38 __ breve (music marking)
39 Make less intense
40 Youngman yuk
41 Mexican statesman Juárez
42 No gentleman
45 CBS symbol
47 Deck out
48 Convene after a break
49 Brings to bear
51 Sour-tasting
53 Harder to come by
56 Sciences' partner
57 Enter
58 Leather attachment?
60 Serenade the moon
61 It may be odd or inside
62 Actress Gardner
64 Yucatan "yay!"

by Bob Lubbers

ACROSS
1 Theater ticket
6 Poet Ogden
10 Comes last
14 Win by __
15 Sandwich cookie
16 Bailiwick
17 __ Monica, CA
18 Big squeeze
20 Beach find
22 Sell via pushcart
23 Sound system
25 *Damn Yankees* character
27 Actor Judd
28 Lawless
33 Decide
34 Destiny
36 "The March King"
37 Busy
39 *Ora pro* __
41 Bundle
42 Bennett and Danza
44 Helen's captor
46 It might be cast
47 Unlike a rookie
49 Hungarian
51 Theda of silents
52 Branches
53 Star in Aquila
57 Niger-Congo language family
58 Type of piano
61 Skylit lobbies
64 "*Dies* __"

65 Smell
66 "I Am Woman" singer
67 Corn units
68 Despicable sort
69 Indo-European

DOWN
1 __ *Boot*
2 Merkel or O'Connor
3 Little squeeze
4 Mary and John Jacob
5 New Jersey town
6 Biblical sailor
7 Circle segment
8 "Wait a __!"

9 Big to-do
10 *Shane* star
11 Dry
12 Earth sci.
13 Of sound mind
19 Does parenting
21 "Over There" composer
23 Young pigs
24 Walk carefully
25 Brazilian dance
26 Studio sign
29 Female whale
30 Cranker
31 Biblical prophet
32 Salad garnishes
35 Cowboy, at times
38 Cobb and Hardin

40 *The Lion King* character
43 Ferber novel
45 Italian town
48 Limited
50 Alley border
53 Rose's boyfriend
54 Zhivago's love
55 Ski lift
56 Approving votes
57 Apt. accommodation
59 Fuss
60 "Neither rain __ sleet . . ."
62 Lupino of *High Sierra*
63 Novelist Rand

by A.J. Santora

ACROSS

1 Tibetan monks
6 Wedding souvenir
11 Murrow's network
14 Sun Valley's state
15 Queenly crown
16 Shaker Ann
17 Fountain treat
19 Scottish "John"
20 Highball ingredient
21 Discounted by
22 Pie filling
23 Early Northwest trading town
26 Cobbling tool
29 Period
30 Yeshiva lang.
31 Barnum, often
33 Start of an Einstein quote
38 Middle of quote
39 End of quote
40 Unsullied
41 Prefix for fix
42 Actor Ayres
43 Old Brit. Airways craft
45 Evolutionary theory
49 Kind of battery: Abbr.
50 Plane-related
52 __-TURN (highway sign)
53 Brit's raincoat
54 Neutralized
58 School at E. Lansing
59 Benedict Arnold's co-conspirator

60 Common commodity?
61 Bar mem.
62 Easy basketball shot
63 Answer a charge

DOWN

1 Celestial scales
2 "All in __ work!"
3 French impressionist
4 Remark of realization
5 Andrew, to Elizabeth
6 Perplexed
7 Mouth pieces
8 Raft wood
9 Swiss canton
10 Framer's need
11 Reaching the top

12 Gary Cooper classic
13 "Return to __" (Elvis tune)
18 Excuse makers
24 Scarlett and Suellen
25 University officers
27 Kenmore competitor
28 Post-riot opportunists
32 Wreath
33 "__ of the Red-Hot Mamas" (Tucker tune)
34 Nearly bald do
35 Having nothing between praenomen and cognomen: Abbr.

36 Mil. letter drop
37 Ski lift
40 Soprano Dale
44 Cronyn's frequent costar
45 Obnoxious one
46 Levenson's __ *Era and Out the Other*
47 "Liberty Bell" composer
48 Toned down
51 Beige shade
54 "Silent" president
55 Get __ for effort
56 Precognition, initially
57 First US state

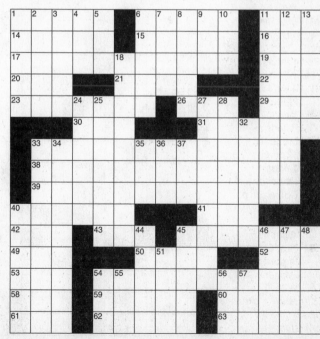

99 COSMIC COLORS

by Randy Sowell

ACROSS
1 Lighting store stock
6 The "it" game
9 Vitality
14 Directive
15 Outer-space omnivore
17 Hardly ever
19 Money drawer
20 By mouth
21 Thesaurus unit: Abbr.
22 Chris of tennis
24 Lon of Cambodia
25 Arizona city
26 Music genre
28 Summer: Fr.
30 Print measures
33 Small stars
39 Measuring device
41 Plaything
42 T.S. __
43 Moon material, supposedly
46 Be nosy
47 Long March leader
48 Tiny circles
50 Paving products
53 Fight-game org.
56 Taking advantage of
59 Compass pt.
60 Wagner works
62 Slithery swimmers
64 Prominent feature of Jupiter
67 With "The," Mars' nickname
68 __ off (forestall)

69 Ore examination
70 Grand __ Opry
71 Stories

DOWN
1 Burglar's take
2 Golfer Palmer, to fans
3 1655, to Caesar
4 Kitchen tool
5 __ Lanka
6 Ski lift
7 British saint
8 Big name in wine
9 __-doke
10 Resistance unit
11 Lodge brother
12 Stratagems
13 Red dye
16 Chose from a group

18 V-shaped cut
23 Mrs. Ivanhoe
25 Breakfast, e.g.
27 __ and kin
29 Sings like the birdies sing
30 Chick-to-be
31 Deface
32 Seek damages from
34 Sock part
35 Looked over
36 Taylor or Torn
37 *A Bell __ Adano*
38 Hog home
40 Prized possessions
44 Southern legume
45 Guzzler

49 Sonora snooze
50 Tropical fish
51 Burning leftovers
52 Marsh growths
54 Number-calling game
55 Soviet cooperative
57 Katmandu's country
58 Hand covering
60 Paris airport
61 Comic Johnson
63 French holy women: Abbr.
65 College transcript initials
66 Summer clock setting: Abbr.

100 NIGHTY-NIGHT

by Norma Steinberg

ACROSS

1 Gent
5 Horn sound
9 Sailboat workers
13 Protagonist
14 Work out the answer
15 Rabbit relative
16 Carried out in secret
18 *Andy Griffith Show* kid
19 Cavern
20 "__ please find . . ."
22 Term of respect
23 Historical periods
25 Leftovers dish
26 __-friendly
27 Cashes in
30 Price
33 Work out a cryptogram
35 French water
36 Word before crust or berth
38 At this moment
39 __ Dame
41 Roofing goo
42 Makes a speech
45 Invites
46 Jacket parts
48 Finch's home
50 Skating jump
51 Farm building
52 Watched the kids
55 Unyielding
58 On the whole
60 Implement
61 1959 Hudson/Day movie
63 Extol
64 Early evening
65 Tom Joad, e.g.
66 Makes a choice
67 Dutch cheese
68 Sties

DOWN

1 Locomotive sounds
2 Monsieur Matisse
3 Enthusiasm
4 Rhymester
5 Scaring word
6 Leprechauns
7 Level
8 Roosted
9 Pick out
10 Police records
11 Smallest Great Lake
12 Dandelion, e.g.
14 Crossed the plate
17 Hwys.
21 Burdened
24 Stadia
26 Southwestern Indian
27 Ivanhoe's bride
28 Hamill or Harmon
29 Brings to court
30 Uses scissors
31 Moonstone
32 Occupying lots of space
34 Portable bed
37 Fido's friend
40 Feedbag grain
43 Backslide
44 Preacher's talk
47 Delights (in)
49 Winter forecast
51 Author Plain
52 Wager
53 Exhausted
54 Youngsters
55 Director Preminger
56 Toon Betty
57 Fit to be __
59 Cease
62 Moon lander

ANSWERS

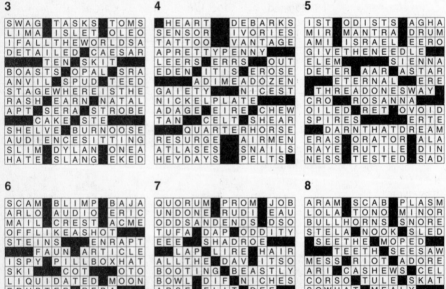

1

```
DEFAME EMS WISP
ADRIAN MOO ETTA
DAILYGRIND EARN
    BLARED KLEE
CRIMEAN YELLOWS
HOLO NTH NAY
AMIN DEAD SLOPE
SEATS RYE TONER
MOCHA SECS TIER
LIN KAT TOTE
BABYLON TALONED
OVER TENURE
DELE YEARLYDUES
ERIN EDT ETERNE
STET TSE TENDON
```

2

```
PANT CASH LASER
IDEA OREO OUTRE
EARLDERRBIGGERS
SMOKER BOSC MST
    ACH SLAW
SAGE IAM ABIDES
OVAL ONUS INEPT
RAYMONDCHANDLER
TILER SHUN OLEO
ALERTS OTT WASP
    SHAM SEZ
ARC ORES RESCUE
JOHNDICKSONCARR
AVISO CIAO ORAL
RETAX ATOM TALE
```

3

```
SWAG TASKS TOMS
LIMA ISLET OLEO
IFALLTHEWORLDSA
DETAILED CAESAR
    TEN SKIT
BOASTS OPAL SRA
ANVIL SPUD TEED
STAGEWHEREISTHE
RASH EARN NATAL
APT SERA STROBE
    CAKE STE
SHELVE BURNOOSE
AUDIENCESITTING
SLIM DYLAN ONEA
HATE SLANG EKED
```

4

```
HEART DEBARKS
SENSOR IVORIES
TATTOO VANTAGE
APRETTYPENNY
LEERS ERRS OUT
EDEN ITIS EROSE
ADIMEADOZEN
GAIETY NICEST
NICKELPLATE
ADAGE EIRE CHEW
TAN CELT SHEAR
QUARTERHORSE
RESURGE AIRMEN
ATLASES SNAILS
HEYDAYS PELTS
```

5

```
IST ODISTS AGHA
MIR MANTRA DRUM
AMI ISRAEL EERO
GIVETHENEEDLE
ELEM SIENNA
DETER AAR ASTAR
ETERNAL ERE
THREADONESWAY
CRO ROSANNA
OILED RET OVOID
SPIRES ERTE
DARNTHATDREAM
ERAS ORATOR ALA
RAYE RUTILE DIN
NESS TESTED SAD
```

6

```
SCAM BLIMP BAJA
ARLO AUDIO ERIC
MAIL CREST ACME
OFFLIKEASHOT
STEINS ENRAPT
FAUN ARTICLE
ISPY PILLBOXHAT
SKI COT OTO
LIQUIDATED MOON
ERUPTED REBA
STEPUP MORGAN
SPACECAPSULE
BELA RADON HAVE
EVIL TRIED AVID
GAZA SLEDS SANS
```

7

```
QUORUM PROM JOB
UNDONE RUDI EAU
ODDSANDENDS DSO
TUFA DAP ODDITY
EEE SHADROE
LAP LIRE HAIR
ALLTHE DAV ITSO
BOOTING BEASTLY
BOWL DIF NICHES
APSE FLIT DEE
EGOTRIP EBB
CENSOR SKI KNEE
RIO BETTINGODDS
URN ANIL GALOOT
ZEE DDAY STAFFS
```

8

```
ARAM SCAB PLASM
LOLA TONO MINOR
BULLHORNS SNORE
STELA NOOK SLED
SEETHE MOPED
TEETH SEESAW
MESS RIOT ADORE
ARI CASHEWS CEL
CORSO TULE SKAT
SOWHAT MEALY
AILEY CRIMPS
PULP NOVA APLEA
ARTOO DESERTERS
TEEUP EATS ONIT
HARTE LUST MANO
```

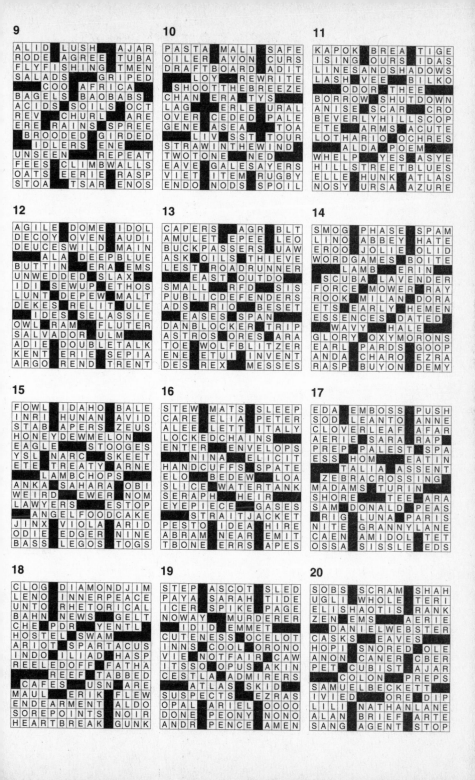

9

A	L	I	D		L	U	S	H		A	J	A	R
R	O	D	E		A	G	R	E	E		T	U	B	A
F	L	Y	F	I	S	H	I	N	G		T	M	E	N
S	A	L	A	D	S			G	R	I	P	E	D
			C	O	O		A	F	R	I	C	A
B	A	G	E	L	S		B	A	O	B	A	B	S
A	C	I	D	S		S	O	I	L	S		O	C	T
R	E	V		C	H	U	R	L		A	R	E
E	R	E		R	A	I	N	S		S	P	R	E	E
B	R	O	O	D	E	D		G	I	R	D	E	D
	I	D	L	E	R	S		E	N	E
U	N	S	E	E	N			R	E	P	E	A	T
F	E	E	S		C	L	I	M	B	W	A	L	L	S
O	A	T	S		E	E	R	I	E		R	A	S	P
S	T	O	A		T	S	A	R		E	N	O	S

10

PASTA MALI SAFE
OILER AVON CURS
DRAFTBOARD ADIT
LOY REWRITE
SHOOTTHEBREEZE
CHAN ERA TYS
LAG ERLE URAL
OVER CEDED PALE
GENE ASEA TOA
LIV SST TOUR
STRAWINTHEWIND
TWOTONE NED
EAVE GALESAYERS
VIET ITEM RUGBY
ENDO NODS SPOIL

11

KAPOK BREA TIGE
ISING OURS IDAS
LINESANDSHADOWS
LASH VEE BILKO
ODOR THEE
BORROW SHUTDOWN
ANISE SCAR CRO
BEVERLYHILLSCOP
ETE ARMS ACUTE
LOTHARIO OCHRES
ALDA POEM
WHELP YES ASYE
HILLSTREETBLUES
ELLE HUNK ATLAS
NOSY URSA AZURE

12

AGILE DOME IDOL
DECOY OVEN AUDI
DEUCESWILD MAIN
ALA DEEPBLUE
BUTTIN ERA EMS
UNWEDDED SLAX
IDI SEWUP ETHOS
LUNT DEPEW MALT
DEKES RELIT ULE
IDES SELASSIE
OWL RAM FLUTER
SALVADOR ULM
ADIE DOUBLETALK
KENT ERIE SEPIA
ARGO REND TRENT

13

CAPERS AGR BLT
AMULET EPEE LEO
BUCKPASSERS UAW
ASK OILS THIEVE
LEST ROADRUNNER
EAST OUTDO
SMALL RFD SIS
PUBLICDEFENDERS
ADS RIO BESET
EASES SPAN
DANBLOCKER TRIP
ASTROS ORES ARA
TOE WOLFBLITZER
ENE ETUI INVENT
DES REX MESSES

14

SMOG PHASE SPAM
LINO ABBEY HATE
EROO JOLIE OLID
WORDGAMES BOITE
LAMB ERIN
SCUBA LAVENDER
FORCE MOWER RAY
ROOK MILAN DORA
ETS EARLY HEMEN
ESSENCES DATED
WAVY HALE
GLORY OXYMORONS
EARL PARDS GOOP
ANDA CHARO EZRA
RASP BUYON DEMY

15

FOWL IDAHO BALE
INRI HUNAN AVID
STAB APERS ZEUS
HONEYDEWMELON
EAGLE STOOGES
YSL NARC SKEET
ETE TREATY ARNE
LAMBCHOPS
ANKA SAHARA OBI
WEIRD EWER NOM
LAWYERS ESTOP
ANGELFOODCAKE
JINX VIOLA ARID
ODIE EDGER NINE
BASS LEGOS TOGS

16

STEW MATS SLEEP
CARE ELIA PETER
ALEE LETT ITALY
LOCKEDCHAINS
ENTER ENVELOPS
NINA ELICIT
HANDCUFFS SPATE
ELO BEDEW LOA
SLICE WATERTANK
SERAPH HEIR
EYEPIECE GASES
STRAITJACKET
PESTO IDEA HIRE
ABRAM NEAR EMIT
TBONE ERRS APES

17

EDA EMBOSS PUSH
SOD LEANTO ANNE
CLOVERLEAF AFAR
AERIE SARA RAP
PREP PALEST SPA
ESS HOM EATIN
TALIA ASSENT
ZEBRACROSSING
MADAMS TURIN
SHORE TEE ARA
SAM DONALD PEAS
RIG LUNA PARIS
NITE GRANNYLANE
CAEN AMIDOL TET
OSSA SISSLE EDS

18

CLOG DIAMONDJIM
LENO INNERPEACE
UNTO RHETORICAL
BAHN NEWS GELT
CHE PDR YENTL
HOSTEL SWAM
ARIOT SPARTACUS
INDO ILIAD HASP
REELEDOFF FATHA
REEF TABBED
CAFES USN ARE
MAUL ERIK FLEW
ENDEARMENT ALDO
SOREPOINTS NOIR
HEARTBREAK GUNK

19

STEP ASCOT SLED
PAYA SARAH TIDE
ICER SPIKE PAGE
NOWAY MURDERER
IDID EMMET
CUTENESS OCELOT
INNS COOL ORONO
VIE NOTFAIR CAW
ITSSO OPUS AKIN
CESTLA ADMIRERS
ATLAS SKID
SUSPECTS EZRAS
OPAL ARIEL OOOO
DONE PEONY NONO
ANDR PENCE AMEN

20

SOBS SCRAM SHAH
UGLI WHOLE TERI
ELISHAOTIS RANK
ZEN EMS AERIE
DANIELWEBSTER
CASKS EAVES
HOPI SNORED OLE
ANON CANER CBER
PET CUBIST AJAR
COLON PREPS
SAMUELBECKETT
IVIED ORE DIP
LILI NATHANLANE
ALAN BRIEF ARTE
SANG AGENT STOP

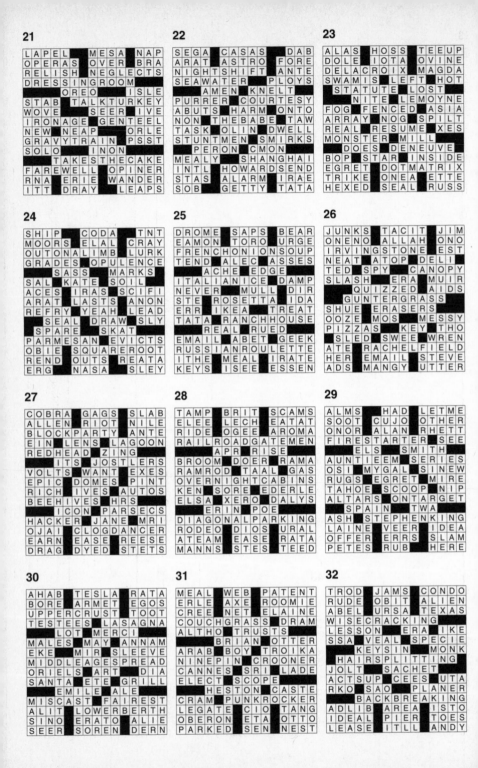

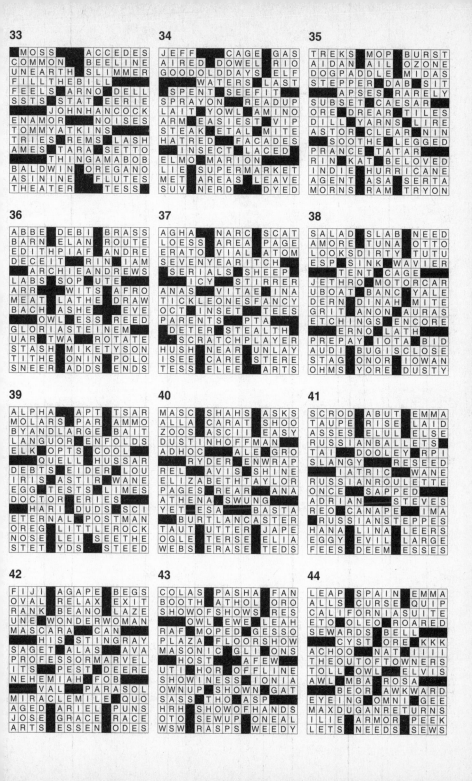

33

```
MOSS    ACCEDES
COMMON  BEELINE
UNEARTH SLIMMER
FILLTHEBILL
FEELS ARNO DELL
SSTS STAT EERIE
  JOHNHANCOCK
ENAMOR  NOISES
TOMMYATKINS
TRIES REMS LASH
AMES TARA SETTO
 THINGAMABOB
BALDWIN OREGANO
ASININE FLUTES
THEATER  TESS
```

34

```
JEFF   CAGE  GAS
AIRED DOWEL  RIO
GOODOLDDAYS  ELF
   WATERS LAST
SPENT  SEEFIT
SPRAYON  READUP
LAIT YOWL AMINO
ARM EASIEST VIP
STEAK ETAL MITE
HATRED  FACADES
 INSECT  LACED
ELMO  MARION
LIE SUPERMARKET
MET AREAS LEAVE
SUV NERD  DYED
```

35

```
TREKS MOP BURST
AIDAN AIL OZONE
DOGPADDLE MIDAS
STEPPER DAB SIT
 APSES  RARELY
SUBSET  CAESAR
ORE DREAR TILES
DILL YARNS LIRE
ASTOR CLEAR NIN
 SOOTHE LEGGED
PRANCE  TATAR
RIN KAT BELOVED
INDIE HURRICANE
AGENT ASA SERTA
MORNS RAM TRYON
```

36

```
ABBE DEBI BRASS
BARN ELAN ROUTE
EDITHPIAF ANDRE
DECEIT RIN IAM
 ARCHIEANDREWS
LABS SOP UTE
ARR  WITS  AFRO
MEAT LATHE DRAW
BACH ASHE  EVE
OWL  ESS  REED
GLORIASTEINEM
UAR TWA ROTATE
STASH MIKETYSON
TITHE ONIN POLO
SNEER ADDS ENDS
```

37

```
AGHA  NARC SCAT
LOESS AREA PAGE
ERATO VIAL ATOM
SEVENYEARITCH
 SERIALS SHEEP
ICY  STIRRER
ANAS VITAE INA
TICKLEONESFANCY
OCT INSET TEES
PARENTS  PTA
DETER STEALTH
 SCRATCHPLAYER
HUSH NEAR UNLAY
ISEE CARE STERE
TESS ELEE  ARTS
```

38

```
SALAD SLAB NEED
AMORE TUNA OTTO
LOOKSDIRTY TUTU
ESP SINK WAVIER
 TENT  CAGE
JETHRO MOTORCAR
UBOAT BANC YALE
DERN DINAH MITE
GRIT ANON AURAS
ETCHINGS ENCORE
ERNO LATH
PREPAY IOTA BID
AUDI BUGISCLOSE
STAG ONOR IOWAN
OHMS YORE DUSTY
```

39

```
ALPHA  APT TSAR
MOLARS PAR AMMO
BYANDLARGE BAIT
LANGUOR ENFOLDS
ELK OPTS  COOL
 QUELL  HUSSAR
DEBTS EIDER LOU
IRIS ASTIR WANE
EGG TESTS LIMES
DOCTOR  ERIES
HARI DUDS SCI
ETERNAL POSTMAN
OREG LITTLEROCK
NOSE LEI SEETHE
STET YDS  STEED
```

40

```
MASC SHAHS ASKS
ALLA CARAT SHOO
ZOOS ASCII EASY
DUSTINHOFFMAN
ADHOC ALE GRO
 RYDER  ENWRAP
REL AVIS SHINE
ELIZABETHTAYLOR
PAGES REAR ANA
ATHENA  SWUNG
YET ESA  BASTA
 BURTLANCASTER
TAUT UTTER JAPE
OGLE TERSE ELIA
WEBS ERASE TEDS
```

41

```
SCROD ABUT EMMA
TAUPE RISE LAID
ASSES ELUL ELSE
RUSSIANBALLETS
TAI DOOLEY RPI
SLANGY  RESEED
 IATRIC  WANE
RUSSIANROULETTE
ONCE  SAPPED
ADRIAN  STEVES
REO CANAPE IMA
RUSSIANSTEPPES
HANA LINA LEERS
EGGY EVIL LARGE
FEES DEEM ESSES
```

42

```
FIJI AGAPE BEGS
OVAL RELAX EXIT
RANK BEANO LAZE
UNE WONDERWOMAN
MASCARA  CAN
 HIS STINGRAY
SAGET ALAS  AVA
PROFESSORMARVEL
ITS  PEST DEERE
NEHEMIAH  FOB
VAL  PARASOL
MIRACLEMILE QUO
AGED ARIEL PUNS
JOSE GRACE RACE
ARTS ESSEN ODES
```

43

```
COLAS PASHA FAN
BOOTH ATHOL ORO
SHOWOFSHOWS RES
 OWL EWE LEAH
RAF MOPED GESSO
PLAZA FLOORSHOW
MASONIC GLI ONS
HOST  AFEW
UTI HOR OFFLINE
SHOWINESS IONIA
OWNUP SHOWN GAT
SASS THO  ASP
HRH SHOWOFHANDS
OTO SEWUP ONEAL
WSW RASPS WEEDY
```

44

```
LEAP SPAIN EMMA
ALLS CURSE QUIP
CALIFORNIASUITE
ETO OLEO ROARED
SEWARDS  BELL
CYST ORE  KKK
ACHOO NAT IIII
THEOUTOFTOWNERS
TOLL OWL ELVIS
AWL MBA  ROSA
 BEOR AWKWARD
EYEING OMNI GEE
MAXDUGANRETURNS
ILIE ARMOR PEEK
LETS NEEDS SEWS
```

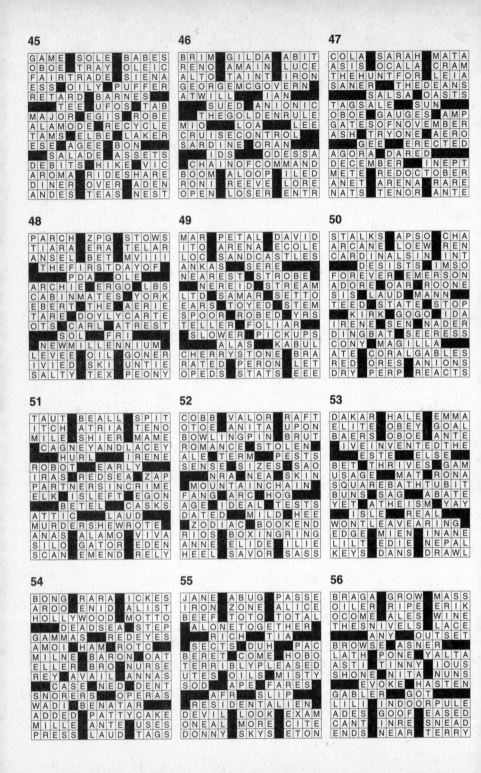

45

```
GAME . SOLE . BABES
OBOE . TRAY . OLEIC
FAIRTRADE . SIENA
ESS . OILY . PUFFER
RETARD . BARNES . .
. . TEE . UFOS . TAB
MAJOR . EGIS . ROBE
ALAMODE . RECYCLE
TAMS . ELBE . LAKER
ESE . AGEE . BON . .
. SALADE . ASSETS .
DEBITS . HIKE . VIC
AROMA . RIDESHARE
DINER . OVER . ADEN
ANDES . TEAS . NEST
```

46

```
BRIM . GILDA . ABIT
RENO . AMAIN . LUCE
ALTO . TAINT . IRON
GEORGEMCGOVERN .
ATWILL . . IAN . . .
. . . SUED . ANIONIC
THEGOLDENRULE . .
MIO . . LOA . . LEE
. CRUISECONTROL .
SARDINE . ORAN . .
. . IDS . . ODESSA
. CHAINOFCOMMAND
BOOM . ALOOP . ILED
RONI . REEVE . LORE
OPEN . LOSER . ENTR
```

47

```
COLA . SARAH . MATA
ASIS . OCALA . CRAM
THEHUNTFOR . LEIA
SANER . . THEDEANS
. . . SALSA . OASTS
TAGSALE . . SUN . .
OBOE . GAUGES . AMP
GATESOFNOVEMBER
ASH . TRYONE . AERO
. . GEE . ERECTED .
AGORA . DARED . . .
DECEMBER . INEPT
METE . REDOCTOBER
ANET . ARENA . RARE
NATS . TENOR . ANTE
```

48

```
PARCH . ZPG . STOWS
TIARA . ERA . TELAR
ANSEL . BET . MVIII
. THEFIRSTDAYOF .
. . . PDA . OLE . . .
ARCHIE . ERGO . LBS
CABINMATES . YORK
EBERT . THE . AERIE
TARE . DOYLYCARTE
OTS . CARL . ATREST
. . . SOL . FRI . . .
. NEWMILLENNIUM .
LEVEE . OIL . GONER
IVIED . SKI . UNTIE
SALTY . TEX . PEONY
```

49

```
MAR . PETAL . DAVID
ITO . ARENA . ECOLE
LOC . SANDCASTLES
ANKAS . SERE . . . .
NEAREST . STROBE .
. NEREID . STREAM .
LTD . SAMAR . SETTO
EARS . TOYED . STEM
SPOOR . ROBED . YRS
TELLER . FOLIAR . .
SLOWER . PICKUPS .
. ALAS . . KABUL . .
CHERRYSTONE . BRA
RATED . PERON . LET
OPEDS . STATS . EEE
```

50

```
STALKS . APSO . CHA
ARCANE . LOEW . REN
CARDINALSIN . INT
. . . DESISTS . IMSO
FOREVER . EMERSON
ADORE . OAR . ROONE
SIS . LAUD . MANN .
TEED . STATE . STOP
. KIRK . GOGO . IDA
IRENE . SEN . NADER
DINGBAT . SEERESS
CONY . MAGILLA . .
ATE . CORALGABLES
RED . ORES . ANIONS
DRY . PERP . REACTS
```

51

```
TAUT . BEALL . SPIT
ITCH . ATRIA . TENO
MILE . SHIER . MAME
. CAGNEYANDLACEY
. . HURL . . IRENE .
ROBOT . EARLY . . .
IRAS . REDSEA . ZAP
PARTNERSINCRIME
ELK . ISLEFT . EGON
. . . BETEL . CASKS
ATTIC . LAUD . . . .
MURDERSHEWROTE .
ANAS . ALAMO . VIVA
SILO . GATOR . EDEN
SCAN . EMEND . RELY
```

52

```
COBB . VALOR . RAFT
OTOE . ANITA . UPON
BOWLINGPIN . BRUT
ROMANCE . STOLEN
ALE . TERM . PESTS
SENSE . SIZES . SAO
. . NRA . NEA . SKIN
. MOUNTAINCHAIN .
FANG . ARC . HOG . .
AGE . IDEAL . TESTS
DATED . MILD . HEE
ZODIAC . BOOKEND
RIOS . BOXINGRING
ANNE . ELIDE . ILIE
HEEL . SAVOR . SASS
```

53

```
DAKAR . HALE . EMMA
ELITE . OBEY . GOAL
BAERS . OBOE . ANTE
. IVEINVENTEDTHE
. . ESTE . . ELSE . .
BET . THRIVES . GAM
USAGE . MAT . RONA
SQUAREBATHTUBIT
BUNS . SAG . ABATE
YET . ATHEISM . YAY
. . ISLE . REAL . . .
WONTLEAVEARING .
EDGE . MIEN . INANE
LILT . EDIE . NEPAL
KEYS . DANS . DRAWL
```

54

```
BONG . RARA . ICKES
AROO . ENID . ALIST
HOLLYWOOD . MOTTO
. . DEADSEA . STEP
GAMMAS . REDEYES
AMOI . HAM . ROTC .
MILNE . BARON . OAT
ELLER . BRO . NURSE
REY . AVAIL . ANNAS
. CASE . NED . DENT
SNORERS . OPERAS .
WADI . BENATAR . .
ADDED . PATTYCAKE
MILLE . ANTE . USES
PRESS . LAUD . TAGS
```

55

```
JANE . ABUG . PASSE
IRON . ZONE . ALICE
BEEF . TOTO . TOTAL
. ALONETOGETHER .
. . RICH . . TIA . . .
SECTS . DUH . PAC .
BERET . COME . HOBO
TERRIBLYPLEASED
UTES . OILS . MISTY
SOD . APE . FARES .
. . . AFR . SLIP . . .
. RESIDENTALIEN .
DEVIL . LOOK . EXAM
ONEAL . MORE . CITE
DONNY . SKYS . ETON
```

56

```
BRAGA . GROW . MASS
OILER . RIPE . ERIK
OCOME . ALES . WINE
THESNIVELS . LACE
. . . ANY . OUTSET
BROWSE . ASNER . .
LATH . PONE . YALTA
ASTI . TINNY . IOUS
SHONE . NITA . NUNS
. . EVOKE . HASTEN
GABLER . GOT . . . .
LILI . INDOORPULE
ADES . GOOF . EASED
CANT . INRE . SNEAD
ENDS . NEAR . TERRY
```

57

S	P	A	R		P	R	A	M		S	O	F	A	R
H	A	L	E		L	O	S	E		I	R	A	T	E
A	L	O	T		A	T	T	A		C	A	L	E	B
N	I	N	E	I	N	C	H	N	A	I	L	S		
A	N	G	L	O	S		E	T	A	L		E	G	O
			L	O	T	T		R	I	C	H	E	R	
C	O	D		F	O	U	R	S	E	A	S	O	N	S
A	M	I	S			R	E	N			T	O	R	O
J	A	C	K	S	O	N	F	I	V	E		D	E	N
	U	N	T	I	E	D		P	E	A	K			
N	I	A		R	I	T	A		G	R	E	E	T	S
	T	H	R	E	E	D	O	G	N	I	G	H	T	
A	R	O	M	A		N	O	W	I		T	R	E	E
P	E	R	O	T		A	B	L	E		H	E	R	E
T	A	S	S	E		M	E	S	S		S	T	E	P

58

	D	E	M	O			S	E	C	U	R	E		
	T	R	U	E	U	P		P	L	A	T	E	N	
S	A	O	R	S	T	A	T	E	I	R	E	A	N	N
L	I	P		H	O	T	H	E	A	D		L	O	O
A	P	I	N		F	E	E	D	S		D	E	B	T
V	E	N	O	M		D	R	S		T	E	S	L	A
S	I	T	T	E	E		M	U	S	E	T	T	E	
		H	E	T	E	R	O	P	T	E	R	A		
S	E	V	E	N	A	M		O	R	A	T	O	R	
F	A	B	E	R		G	E	T		S	C	E	N	E
I	R	U	N		F	S	T	O	P		T	A	C	S
A	S	C		H	E	H	E	A	R	D		G	E	E
T	A	K	E	I	T	O	R	L	E	A	V	E	I	T
	R	E	W	R	A	P		L	E	M	O	N	S	
	S	T	E	E	L	S			N	E	X	T		

59

P	A	S	T	A		H	E	R			S	E	A	S
A	C	H	E	D		E	R	I	N		E	L	S	E
C	R	E	A	M		A	N	D	I		D	I	K	E
T	E	L		I	N	D	E	E	P	W	A	T	E	R
			L	U	R	E	S		P	I	N	E	D	
R	U	S	S	E	T			G	L	E	N	S		
A	L	O	E		S	T	R	I	D	E		S	O	B
I	N	U	R	E		R	A	N		S	T	A	G	E
N	A	T		D	O	U	B	T	S		K	N	E	E
			D	I	N	E	S		E	R	O	D	E	S
	S	K	A	T	E			G	R	A	S	P		
S	U	N	S	H	I	N	E	L	A	W		A	A	H
A	M	A	H		D	A	L	I		E	M	P	T	Y
R	A	V	E		A	S	A	N			S	P	E	E	D
A	C	E	S			A	L	T			T	H	R	E	E

60

B	A	S	H		B	E	T	T	E		P	F	F	T
O	B	O	E		A	L	I	E	N		L	I	R	E
B	E	A	R	B	R	Y	A	N	T		E	L	E	E
S	T	R	A	I	N	S		D	R	E	A	M	E	D
			L	A	S		P	E	E	R	S			
L	E	N	D	S		T	A	R		R	U	B	E	S
I	V	E			A	E	R		S	O	R	E	L	Y
M	E	A	D	O	W	L	A	R	K	L	E	M	O	N
E	N	T	I	R	E		D	A	Y		A	P	O	
S	T	O	O	D		M	E	G		P	O	S	E	D
			R	E	G	I	S		A	L	P			
S	H	E	A	R	E	R		P	E	O	P	L	E	S
T	E	A	M		T	I	G	E	R	W	O	O	D	S
U	R	S	A		M	A	O	R	I		S	L	I	T
B	O	Y	S		E	M	O	T	E		E	A	T	S

61

T	H	U	M	P		Y	A	R	D		G	U	S	H
R	A	T	I	O		I	S	E	E		I	G	O	R
E	L	I	O	T		P	I	E	F	I	G	H	T	S
E	E	L		A	S	P		L	E	N	O			
D	R	E	S	S	L	E	R			A	R	L	E	N	E
			T	H	R	E	E	S	T	O	O	G	E	S
L	A	Y			V	I	S	A			G	E	T	
S	A	B	E	R		T	A	X		D	I	O	D	E
O	P	A		I	C	B	M		A	N	Y			
	F	A	C	E	S	L	A	P	P	I	N	G		
A	Z	A	L	E	A		S	A	V	I	O	U	R	S
	A	T	N	O		N	Y	E		N	E	T		
E	Y	E	P	O	K	I	N	G		C	E	D	A	R
L	U	G	S		E	L	I	E		E	L	U	D	E
F	L	O	E		D	Y	A	D		S	L	E	E	P

62

F	R	A	C	A	S		T	O	A	D		A	R	P
I	N	L	O	V	E		O	D	I	E		V	E	E
B	A	L	L	A	D	O	P	E	R	A		O	P	E
			L	A	N	E			R	I	C	E	R	
R	E	W	R	O	T	E		R	A	S	C	A	L	S
E	L	A	I	N	E		C	O	P	I	E	D		
E	L	L	A		D	A	U	B	E	R		O	D	D
S	I	D	L	E		U	T	E		S	U	P	E	R
O		E	S	O		C	A	R	E	S	S		R	E	N	O
			P	I	L	L	A	R		L	E	G	A	T	O
S	P	E	C	I	E	S		H	O	V	E	R	E	D
P	O	P	U	P			W	A	W	A				
A	L	P		S	T	E	A	M	E	D	O	P	E	N
R	A	E		E	A	R	L		S	E	L	E	N	A
E	R	R		D	E	A	L		T	R	E	N	D	Y

63

A	M	P	S		C	P	A	S		A	F	L	O	W
S	O	L	E		S	A	L	E		T	R	O	T	H
A	N	A	L	E	P	T	I	C		T	E	S	T	Y
P	A	N	A	M	A	H	A	T	T	I	E			
I	C	E		E	N	E		O	R	C	H	A	R	D
N	O	S	I	R		T	A	R	E			R	O	Y
			N	I	P	I	N		A	T	E	A	S	E
K	E	N	T	U	C	K	Y	D	E	R	B	Y		
M	E	M	O	I	R		L	A	S	S	O			
A	R	I			I	D	E	M		T	O	R	C	H
I	N	T	E	R	N	E		M	O	B		A	R	A
			B	E	A	N	I	E	B	A	B	I	E	S
A	B	A	B	A		T	O	R	O	N	A	D	O	S
C	E	D	E	D		A	T	E	E		F	E	L	L
T	E	D	D	Y		L	A	D	S		F	R	E	E

64

A	T	M		B	E	Y			R	A	C	I	N	G
D	I	O	C	E	S	E		A	M	E	L	I	A	
O	R	D	I	N	A	L		G	A	L	A	X	Y	
B	O	U	N	D	U	P	W	I	T	H				
E	S	S	E			A	N	A		R	O	M	P	
			S	P	R	I	N	G	F	E	V	E	R	
B	A	G		T	A	U	T			A	B	A	T	E
A	I	L	M	E	N	T		S	E	D	A	T	E	S
N	O	M	A	N		S	E	R	E		E	D	S	
J	U	M	P	O	N	B	O	A	R	D				
O	D	E	S		E	A	U		S	T	A	R		
			L	E	A	P	O	F	F	A	I	T	H	
G	N	A	W	E	D		F	L	A	G	D	A	Y	
A	E	R	I	A	L		F	I	R	E	A	R	M	
S	E	E	T	H	E		S	T	E		L	I	E	

65

B	O	T	H		U	S	E	D		T	R	I	P	E
A	T	O	M		N	A	T	E		H	O	L	E	S
T	H	R	O	W	S	T	H	E	B	O	O	K	A	T
H	E	R	S	H	E	Y		P	A	R	T	A	K	E
			E	R	E		Y	A	R	D		R	N	S
	A	N	T			E	B	B	S		T	E	E	
S	C	H	M	O		F	L	U	E		J	U	L	Y
C	H	A	P	T	E	R	A	N	D	V	E	R	S	E
A	I	M	S		D	A	Y	S		I	R	K	E	D
M	P	S		C	I	T	E		A	S	K			
			B	O	S		D	A	T	A		S	M	A
S	L	E	E	P	O	N		C	H	E	A	P	E	N
P	U	T	S	I	N	A	G	O	O	D	W	O	R	D
A	G	R	E	E		P	E	R	M		O	K	I	E
M	E	E	T	S		S	O	N	E		L	E	T	S

66

F	O	O	D		G	R	A	B		S	O	F	A
L	A	N	E	S		L	E	S	E		T	S	A	R
I	T	S	A	T		E	A	T	S		O	U	R	S
T	H	E	D	A	W	N	P	A	T	R	O	L		
	S	T	E	V	E	N	S		I	L	L	S		
			N	E	T		C	E	L	S	I	U	S	
A	G	U	E		S	T	E	A	L		V	E	E
S	U	N	R	I	S	E	S	E	R	E	N	A	D	E
I	M	P		C	A	T	E	S		O	N	E	R
T	U	R	E	E	N	S		N	A	V				
	P	E	R	U		C	O	N	T	E	N	D		
			S	E	P	T	E	M	B	E	R	M	O	R	N
B	O	S	C		A	L	D	O		A	B	B	I	E
A	B	E	T		L	I	R	E		S	E	L	E	S
L	I	D	S		L	E	S	S		R	E	D	S

67

H	E	R	B		S	K	I	D		S	T	U	D	S
O	L	E	O		W	O	R	E		O	U	N	C	E
R	A	P	T		E	R	I	E		O	L	D	I	E
S	T	O	C	K	R	E	S	P	O	N	S	E		
E			Y	E	S	H	I	V	A		R	E	A	R	M	S
			E	T	E		S	T	I	R		T	A	P
L	A	D	E		S	L	U	E		S	A	K	I
S	E	C	U	R	I	T	Y	B	L	A	N	K	E	T
H	T	T	P		V	A	L	E		M	A	E	S
A	G	O		W	I	R	Y		O	A	K			
	M	O	N	R	O	E		A	B	S	E	N	C	E
			B	O	N	D	J	A	M	E	S	B	O	N	D
F	R	E	U	D		E	S	P	Y		I	W	O	N
B	I	L	G	E		T	A	L	E		T	A	T	A
I	D	L	E	R		S	P	E	D		E	Y	E	S

68

H	A	H	A	S		V	O	L	T		S	I	L	O
A	G	E	N	T		E	V	E	R		P	R	A	T
L	E	R	O	I		R	I	T	A		L	O	N	I
F	R	O	M	C	T	O	S	H	I	N	I	N	G	C
			I	K	O	N		A	L	O	T			
C	E	D	E		R	I	L	L		W	O	E	B	E
R	P	O		M	A	C	E		L	I	F	T	E	R
I	O	N	L	Y	H	A	V	E	I	S	F	O	R	U
S	C	H	U	S	S		E	S	T	E		N	I	P
P	H	O	N	O		A	R	C	H		I	S	A	T
			C	R	A	N		A	E	O	N			
O	N	T	H	E	G	O	L	D	B	R	I	C	K	
P	O	R	E		A	L	I	A		E	O	S	I	N
A	G	I	O		K	I	L	T		A	M	I	N	E
L	O	O	N		E	A	S	E		H	E	N	C	E

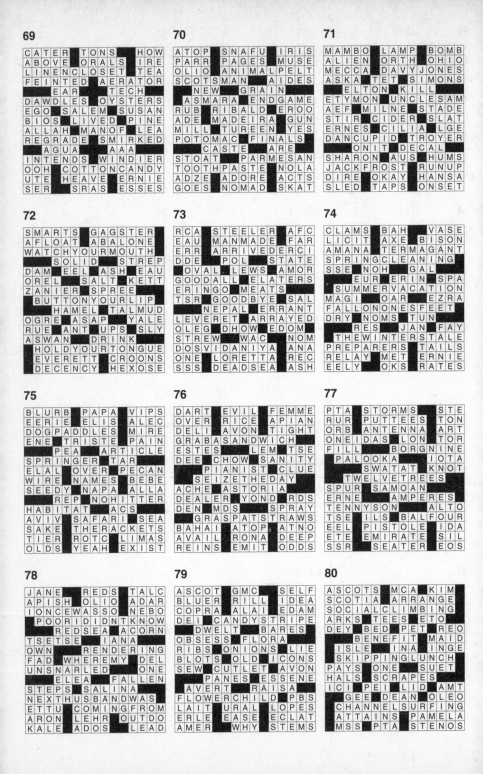

69

```
CATER TONS  HOW
ABOVE ORALS IRE
LINENCLOSET TEA
FEINTED AERATOR
    EAR   TECH
DAWDLES OYSTERS
EGO SALEM SUSAN
BIOS LIVED PINE
ALLAH MANOF LEA
REGRADE SMIRKED
  AGUA   AAA
INTENDS WINDIER
OOH COTTONCANDY
UTE HEAVE ERNIE
SER SRAS  ESSES
```

70

```
ATOP SNAFU IRIS
PARR PAGES MUSE
OLIO ANIMALPELT
SCOTSMAN  AIDES
   NEW  GRAIN
ASMARA ENDGAME
RUB RIBALD EROO
ADE MADEIRA GUN
MILL TUREEN YES
POTOMAC FINALS
   CASTE  ARE
STOAT  PARMESAN
TOOTHPASTE NOLA
ADZE ADORE ACTS
GOES NOMAD SKAT
```

71

```
MAMBO LAMP BOMB
ALIEN ORTH OHIO
MECCA DAVYJONES
ASKA TET SIMONS
   ELTON  KILL
ETYMON UNCLESAM
AEF MILNE STADE
STIR CIDER SLAT
ERNES CILIA LGE
DANCUPID TROYER
   ONIT  DECAL
SHARON AUS HUMS
JACKFROST RUNUP
DIRE OKAY HANSA
SLED TAPS ONSET
```

72

```
SMARTS  GAGSTER
AFLOAT  ABALONE
WATCHYOURMOUTH
  SOLID   STREP
DAM EEL ASH EAU
OREL SALT KETT
ZANIER  SPREE
BUTTONYOURLIP
HAMEL  TALMUD
OGRE ASAP YALE
RUE ANT UPS SLY
ASWAN   DRINK
HOLDYOURTONGUE
EVERETT CROONS
DECENCY HEXOSE
```

73

```
RCA STEELER AFC
EAU MANMADE FAR
ERR ARRIVEDERCI
DDE POL  STATE
OVAL LEWS  AMOR
GOODALL ELATERS
ERINGO  MEATS
TSR GOODBYE SAL
NEPAL  ERRANT
LEVERET ARRAYED
OLEG DHOW  EDOM
STREW WAC  NOM
DOSVIDANIYA ANA
ONE LORETTA REC
SSS DEADSEA ASH
```

74

```
CLAMS BAH  VASE
LICIT AXE BISON
AMANA TERMAGANT
SPRINGCLEANING
SSE  NOH   GAL
   EUR ERIN SPA
SUMMERVACATION
MAGI  OAR  EZRA
FALLONONESFEET
DRY NOMS   TUN
   RES JAN FAY
THEWINTERSTALE
PREPARERS TAILS
RELAY MET ERNIE
EELY OKS  RATES
```

75

```
BLURB PAPA VIPS
EERIE ELIS ALEC
DOGPADDLES MIRE
ENE TRISTE PAIN
   PEA ARTICLE
SPRINGER  TAR
ELAL OVER PECAN
WIRE NAMES BEBE
SEEDY NAPA ALLA
   REP NOHITTER
HABITAT  ACS
AVIV SAFARI SEA
SAKE THERACKETS
TIER ROTC LIMAS
OLDS YEAH EXIST
```

76

```
DART EVIL FEMME
OVER RICE APIAN
DELI AVON TIGHT
GRABASANDWICH
ESTES LEM  TSE
DEE CHOW SANITY
  PIANIST CLUE
  SEIZETHEDAY
ACHE  ASTORIA
DEALER YOND RDS
DEN MDS  SPRAY
  GRASPATSTRAWS
BAHAI ATOP ATNO
AVAIL RONA DEEP
REINS EMIT ODDS
```

77

```
PTA STORMS  STE
RUR PUTTEES TON
ORB ANTENNA ART
ONEIDAS LON TOR
FILL  BORGNINE
PALOOKA   IOTA
  SWATAT KNOT
  TWELVETREES
SPUR SAMOAN
ERNE  AMPERES
TENNYSON  ALTO
TSE ILS BALFOUR
EEL PISTOLE IDA
ETE EMIRATE SIL
SSR SEATER EOS
```

78

```
JANE  REDS  TALC
APISH OLIO ADAR
IONCEWASSO NEBO
POORIDIDNTKNOW
REDSEA  ACORN
TSETSE  IANA
OWN  RENDERING
FAD WHEREMI DEL
UNSNARLED  ONE
ELEA  FALLEN
STEPS  SALINA
NEXTHUSBANDWAS
ETTU COMINGFROM
ARON LEHR OUTDO
KALE ADOS  LEAD
```

79

```
ASCOT GMC  SELF
BLUER RILL IDEA
COPRA ALAI EDAM
DEI CANDYSTRIPE
DWELT  BARES
OBSESS  FLORA
RIBS ONIONS LIE
BLOTS OLD ICONS
SEW CUTLET AVON
PANES  ESSENE
AVERT  RAISA
FLOWERCHILD PBS
LAIT URAL LOPES
ERLE EASE ECLAT
AMER WHY  STEMS
```

80

```
ASCOTS MCA  KIM
SCOTIA ARRANGE
SOCIALCLIMBING
ARKS TEES  ETO
DEY BED PET REO
BENEFIT   MAID
ISLE  INA  INGE
SKIPPINGLUNCH
PAYS ONE   SUET
HALS  SCRAPES
ICI PEI LID AMT
GEE DEAN   OLEO
CHANNELSURFING
ATTAINS PAMELA
MSS PTA STENOS
```

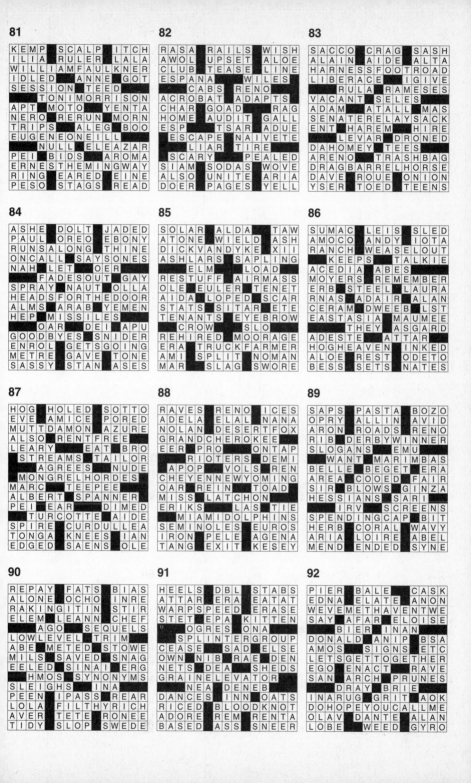

81

KEMP SCALP ITCH
ILIA RULER LALA
WILLIAMFAULKNER
IDLED ANNE GOT
SESSION TEED
TONIMORRISON
APT MOTO YENTA
NERO RERUN MORN
TRIPS ALEG BOO
EUGENEONEILL
NULL ELEAZAR
PEI BIDS AROMA
ERNESTHEMINGWAY
RING EARED EINE
PESO STAGS READ

82

RASA RAILS WISH
AWOL UPSET ALOE
CLUB TEASE LINE
ESPANA WILES
CABS RENO
ACROBAT ADAPTS
CHAR GOAD RAG
HOME AUDIT GALL
ESP TSAR ADUE
ESCAPE NAIVETE
LIAR TIRE
SCARY PEALED
SIAM SODAS WOVE
ALSO UNITE ARIA
DOER PAGES YELL

83

SACCO CRAG SASH
ALAIN AIDE ALTA
HARNESSFOOTROAD
LIBERACE IGIVE
RULA RAMESES
VACANT SELES
ADAM ATALL MAS
SENATERELAYSACK
ENT HAREM HIRE
LEVAR DRONED
DAHOMEY TEES
ARENO TRASHBAG
DRAGBARRELHORSE
DAVE ROUE ONION
YSER TOED TEENS

84

ASHE DOLT JADED
PAUL OREO EBONY
RUNSALONG THINE
ONCALL SAYSONES
NAH LET OER
FADESOUT GAY
SPRAY NAUT OLLA
HEADSFORTHEDOOR
ALMS ARAB YEMEN
HEP MISSILES
OAR DEI APU
GOODBYES SNIDER
ENROL GETSGOING
METRE GAVE TONE
SASSY STAN ASES

85

SOLAR ALDA TAW
ATONE WIELD ASH
DICKVANDYKE XII
ASHLARS SAPLING
ELM LOAD
RESTUFF AIRMASS
OLE EULER TENET
AIDA LOPED SCAR
STATS SITAR ETE
TENANTS EYEBROW
CROW SLO
REHIRED MOORAGE
ERA TRUCKFARMER
AMI SPLIT NOMAN
MAR SLAG SWORE

86

SUMAC LEIS SLED
AMOCO ANDY IOTA
RANCH WEASELOUT
KEEPS TALKIE
ACEDIA ABES
MOYERS REMEMBER
ERB STEEL LAURA
RNAS ADAIR ALAN
CERAM DWEEB LST
EASTASIA MAUMEE
THEY ASGARD
ADESTE ATTAR
HOGHEAVEN INKED
ALOE REST ODETO
BESS SETS NATES

87

HOG HOLED SOTTO
EVE AMICE PORED
MUTTDAMON AZURE
ALSO RENTFREE
LEARY EAT BRO
STREAMS TAILOR
AGREES NUDE
MONGRELHORDES
MARC TEEPEE
ALBERT SPANNER
PEI EAR DIMED
TURCOTTE AIDE
SPIRE CURDULLEA
TONGA KNEES IAN
EDGED SAENS OLE

88

RAVES RENO ICES
ADELA ELAL NANA
NOLAN DESERTFOX
GRANDCHEROKEE
EER PRO ONTAP
RIOTERS DEMI
APOP VOLS REN
CHEYENNEWYOMING
OAR REIN TOAD
MISS LATCHON
ERIKS LAS TIE
MIAMIDOLPHINS
SEMINOLES EUROS
IRON PELE AGENA
TANG EXIT KESEY

89

SAPS PASTA BOZO
OPRY ALLIN AVID
ARON ROADS RENO
RIB DERBYWINNER
SLOGANS EMU
WANT MARIMBAS
BELLE BEGET ERA
AREA COOED FAIR
SIR BLOWS GINZA
HESSIANS SARI
IRV SCREENS
SPENDINGCAP BIT
HERB CORAL WAVY
ARIA LOIRE ABEL
MEND ENDED SYNE

90

REPAY FATS BIAS
ALONE OCHO INRE
RAKINGITIN STIR
ELEM LEANN CHEF
AGO SEQUELS
LOWLEVEL TRIM
ABE METED STOWE
MILS SAVED SNAG
EELED SINAI ERG
HMOS SYNONYMS
SLEIGHS INA
PEEN IPASS REAR
LOLA FILTHYRICH
AVER TETE RONEE
TIDY SLOP SWEDE

91

HEELS DBL STABS
ATTAR ERA EATAT
WARPSPEED ERASE
STET EPA KITTEN
OGRES ONA
SPLINTERGROUP
CEASE SAD ELSE
OWN NIB RAE DEN
NETS DEA SHEDS
GRAINELEVATOR
NEA DENEB
DANCES INN OATS
RICED BLOODKNOT
ADORE REM RENTA
BASED ASS SNEER

92

PIER BALE CASK
EDNA ELATE ANON
WEVEMETHAVENTWE
SAY AFAR ELOISE
BIER INAN
DONALD ANIP BSA
AMOS SIGNS ETC
LETSGETTOGETHER
EGO ENACT RAVE
SAN ARCH PRUNES
DRAY BRIE
INARUG GRIT AOK
DOHOPEYOUCALLME
OLAV DANTE ALAN
LOBE WEED GYRO

93

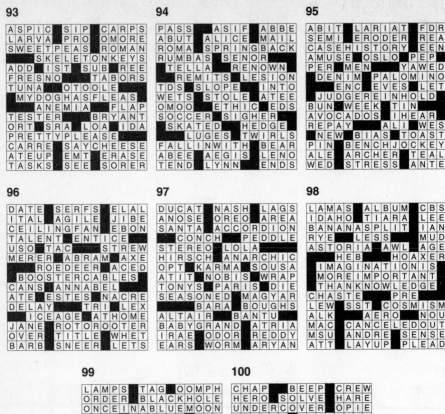

ASPIC·SIP·CARPS
LARVA·PRO·OMORE
SWEETPEAS·ROMAN
··SKELETONKEYS·
ADD·IST·SUB·REE
FRESNO···TABORS
TUNA··OTOOLE···
·MYDOGHASFLEAS·
···ANEMIA··FLAP
TESTER···BRYANT
ORT·SRA·LOA·IDA
·PRETTYPLEASE··
CARRE·SAYCHEESE
ATEUP·EMT·ERASE
TASKS·SEE·SORER

94

PASS··ASIF·ABBE
ABUT·ALICE·MAIL
ROMA·SPRINGBACK
RUMBAS·SENOR···
·TELLA·RENOWN··
··REMITS·LESION
TDS·SLOPE·INTO·
WETS·STOLE·ATEE
OMOO·ETHIC·EDS·
SOCCER·SIGHER··
··SKATED·HEDGE·
···LUGES·TWIRLS
FALLINWITH·BEAR
ABEE·AEGIS·LENO
TEND·LYNN·ENDS

95

ABIT·LARIAT·FDR
SEMI·ERODER·REA
CASEHISTORY·EEN
AMUSE·OSLO·PEP·
PER·MEN··YAWED·
DENIM·PALOMINO·
··ENC·EVES·LET·
·JUDGEREINHOLD·
·BUN·WEEK·TIN··
·AVOCADOS·IHEAR
REPAY·ALI··WES·
NEW·BIAS·TOAST·
PIN·BENCHJOCKEY
ALE·ARCHER·TEAL
WED·STRESS·ANTE

96

DATE·SERFS·ELAL
ITAL·AGILE·JIBE
CEILINGFAN·EBON
TALENT·ENTICE··
USO·TAC··STREW·
MERER·ABRAM·AXE
·ROEDEER··ACED·
·BOOSTERCABLES·
CANS··ANNABEL··
ATE·ESTES·NACRE
DELAY··TRI·LEX·
·ICEAGE·ATHOME·
JANE·ROTOROOTER
OVER·TITLE·WHET
BARB·SNEER·LETS

97

DUCAT·NASH·LAGS
ANOSE·OREO·AREA
SANTA·ACCORDION
·CONCH··PEDDLE·
STEREO·LOLA····
HIRSCH·ANARCHIC
OPT·KARMA·SOUSA
ATIT·NOBIS·WRAP
TONYS·PARIS·DIE
SEASONED·MAGYAR
····BARA·BOUGHS
·ALTAIR··BANTU·
BABYGRAND·ATRIA
IRAE·ODOR·REDDY
EARS·WORM·ARYAN

98

LAMAS·ALBUM·CBS
IDAHO·TIARA·LEE
BANANASPLIT·IAN
RYE··LESS··MUD·
ASTORIA·AWL·AGE
···HEB···HOAXER
·IMAGINATIONIS·
·MOREIMPORTANT·
·THANKNOWLEDGE·
CHASTE···PRE···
LEW·SST·COSMISM
ALK··AERO··NOU·
MAC·CANCELEDOUT
MSU·ANDRE·SENSE
ATT·LAYUP·PLEAD

99

LAMPS·TAG·OOMPH
ORDER·BLACKHOLE
ONCEINABLUEMOON
TILL·ORALLY·SYN
·EVERT·NOL·MESA
···ROCK··ETE···
EMS·WHITEDWARFS
GAUGE·TOY·ELIOT
GREENCHEESE·PRY
···MAO··DOTS···
TARS·WBA·USING·
ESE·OPERAS·EELS
THEGREATREDSPOT
REDPLANET·STAVE
ASSAY·OLE·TALES

100

CHAP··BEEP·CREW
HERO·SOLVE·HARE
UNDERCOVER·OPIE
GROTTO·ENCLOSED
SIR·ERAS··HASH·
··USER·REDEEMS·
COST·DECODE·EAU
UPPER·NOW·NOTRE
TAR·ORATES·ASKS
·SLEEVES·NEST··
·AXEL·BARN·SAT·
OBDURATE·MOSTLY
TOOL·PILLOWTALK
TOUT·SEVEN·OKIE
OPTS·EDAM·PENS